SPEAK UP, LISTEN DOWN

SPEAK UP, LISTEN DOWN

*Finding the courage to challenge
and the humility to learn:
perspectives from 30 years in the police service*

David Howell

Couper Street Books is a publishing brand involved in the professional production and publication management of books. All rights and responsibilities for the contents of this publication remain with the author.

001

Copyright © David Howell, 2023

The moral right of the author has been asserted in accordance with the Copyright, Designs and Patents Act 1988.

All quotes and books are credited within the text where they appear. Any omissions or inaccuracies in the form of credits are unintentional and corrections may be made to future printings.

All rights reserved.

No part of this publication may be reproduced, stored in a retrieval system, or transmitted in any form or by any means, electronic, mechanical, photocopying, recording or otherwise, except as permitted by the UK Copyright, Designs and Patents Act 1988 without the prior permission in writing of the author, nor be otherwise circulated in any form or binding of cover other than that in which it is published and without a similar condition including this condition being imposed on the subsequent purchaser. Designations used by companies to distinguish their products are often claimed as trademarks. All brand names and product names used in this book are trade names, service marks, trademarks or registered trademarks of their respective owners. Neither the publishing brand nor the author is professionally associated with any product or vendor mentioned in this book.

Cover design: Couper Street Books
Typeset by Couper Street Type Company

First published worldwide in 2023

A CIP catalogue record for this book is available from the British Library

ISBN (HB) 978-1-9993477-5-8
ISBN (TPB) 978-1-9993477-4-1
ISBN (e-book) 978-1-9993477-8-9

www.couperstreetbooks.com
www.ableandrush.com

For my mother,

and for

Abby, Elsie and Izzy

PREFACE

I was motivated to write about my experiences in the police, what led me there and how I've used my acquired knowledge since, because I felt I'd had an interesting and, to some extent, a unique career path. I thought my insights might be useful to people within the police and in other walks of life. But, on a personal level, I was also motivated to share the good times and the bad times experienced during my 30 years of policing as a written legacy for my three daughters: Abby, Elsie and Izzy. They were too young at the time, to understand the nature of the role that I performed, and the highs and lows that came with it, and all the associated the risks and rewards. I hope it will give them a new perspective on what those 30 years entailed, and how I was affected, both physically and mentally.

My 30 years of service followed a career trajectory that was highly unusual and thus probably won't ever be experienced again. I regularly reflect on many situations that I found myself in – from training the army and police in Jamaica to flying with the U.S. President's iconic security detail and marvel at how I ended up in them. That said, as I went through the process of recording my experiences, it occurred to me that there was something more to say; a pressing issue I wanted to try to address.

By 2022, policing in the UK seemed to have come to a critical crossroads with public trust and officer morale on the line – both damaged due to high-profile scandals and negative events. As a born problem solver, I thought I could contribute to the conversation with this book. I felt I could offer an interesting perspective from both inside and outside the world of policing.

As with many professional sectors and society on the whole, policing has become increasingly more complex and demanding. Many societal issues have led to heightened conflict, we are surrounded by incompetent leadership and toxic environments, and we have an alarming rise in mental-health issues. The police are not exempt from experiencing any of these. However, I like to remain optimistic and I do believe there are solutions.

The journey to finding any solution for any problem starts with increased self-awareness. And after that, you need good communication skills. But communication includes listening as well as talking, and I have begun to believe that improvements can only be found when those at the "top" of the management structure start to listen more, and those at the "bottom" start to speak up more. It will take courage, humility and vision, but I do believe that the key to a psychologically healthier environment in the workplace starts with speaking up and listening "down".

David Howell
June 2022

CONTENTS

Prologue: Defend The Police		1
Introduction		7

PART ONE:
Learning: A 30-Year Police Career 15

Chapter 1:	Not in the Navy Now	17
Chapter 2:	White Gloves and Bloody Noses	33
Chapter 3:	Stokies Past and Present	42
Chapter 4:	PC Howell	66
Chapter 5:	Traffic on the Ground	76
Chapter 6:	Hold My Fire	94
Chapter 7:	Tragedy Comes With the Job... and With Life	101
Chapter 8:	Traffic from the Air	112
Chapter 9:	A New Perspective	129
Chapter 10:	Flying Further Afield	143
Chapter 11:	Air Operations Unit Identity Crisis	160
Chapter 12:	A Bird's Eye View of London	169
Chapter 13:	A Toxic Ending and New Beginnings	183

PART TWO:
Listening: Creating a Culture of Psychological Safety 191

Chapter 14:	What's the Worst That Could Happen?	193
Chapter 15:	Why Do the Wrong People End Up at the Top?	199

| Chapter 16: | Why Do Good People Get Left Behind? | 204 |
| Chapter 17: | How Do We Become Better Listeners? | 209 |

PART THREE:
Speaking: A Post-Police Career in Consulting — 215

Chapter 18:	Change Management and Conduct Change	217
Chapter 19:	Self-Awareness	222
Chapter 20:	Human Analytics – A Personal User Manual?	230

Epilogue: The Future of Policing — 241

PROLOGUE:

DEFEND THE POLICE

Policing society is not an easy task at the best of times; it is always complex. But in times of turmoil, it can become particularly challenging and stressful. For a long time, I believed there existed a healthy respect between the police in the UK and the people they serve because our tradition, in the UK, is "policing by consent". This is why I found it disturbing to witness an increasingly negative portrayal of the police in the media. It is a topic I feel compelled to speak up about.

London's first professional police force, which replaced the informal and unstructured community-organised service that had existed for several centuries, was established in 1829 by the then Home Secretary, Sir Robert Peel. He wrote the "Peelian Principles", one of which states: *"Police, at all times, should maintain a relationship with the public that gives reality to the historic tradition that the police are the public and the public are the police; the police being only members of the public who are paid to give full-time attention to duties which are incumbent on every citizen in the interests of community welfare and existence."* This acknowledges that there is a tacit understanding that the true power in any liberal democracy lies with the people, and that the people entrust trained police officers to keep the peace. Simply put, the people *consent* to the police having the right to use their judgement to ensure that the laws of the land are enforced.

There is an expectation that police will adhere to the laws of the land, and will not break laws, or be complicit in any injustices. There is an onus on police to ensure that everything they do is fair, above board, and appropriate. We must acknowledge that human beings are not infallible, and mistakes can happen, but we trust that those responsible will acknowledge and apologise for their mistakes and do their best to put them right.

The majority of police officers I have met during my life – both those I have encountered in my civilian life and those I've worked with – have struck me as being good, honest people. You can obviously get bad pennies in all professions. When they turn up in professions where they have considerable power over people, it can be particularly alarming, which is why we need additional vigilance and care in our recruitment processes and supervisory systems: robust checks and balances. We need to find new and innovative processes that will reveal the innate talents that we are all born with and that are honed over our lifetimes, so that we really know who we are, ourselves, and who we are dealing with. Greater self-awareness will protect both police officers and the public they are dealing with. We need to start that reform immediately. The people we recruit today will ultimately go on to be future police leaders and the future face of policing.

No process or system can get it 100% right when dealing with the complexity of human beings, but we must try; we must do our best. We have to keep the faith that the majority of people who are recruited into the police service, and who rise up the hierarchy of the police structure, are good people and suited to their role.

We have to accept that policing is in a constant state of change as it is subjected to internal and external pressures. And people change too. As soon as a new recruit tries on their uniform for the very first time, they know that life will never be the same again; that they will have a new lens to look through. Becoming a police officer gives a person power and authority, and it is critical that this gets used in a fair and conscientious manner if police officers are to build trust and respect with the public. We must never forget how fragile trust is; it is extremely hard and time consuming to build and so easily and quickly shattered.

I believe that a well organised and trusted police service is essential for maintaining order in society. This is why I was so devastated when I started to read and hear the words "DEFUND THE POLICE" again and again, starting in 2020. Every time I saw or heard these words, I wanted to change the "U" to an "E" and persuade people to rethink their attitude and *defend* the police. I don't think people realize how destructive it would be to society if there was no official police service.

The deeply negative attitude towards the police seems to come from a myopic focus, in the media – both the mainstream media and social media platforms – on some isolated incidents; most of which took place in the United States. People pick up on online trends and repeat them without understanding the complexities of the actual incidents or looking behind the headlines and asking probing questions about what might be driving certain news items.

When we zoom in on one incident, or one issue, or one aspect of a problem, we can lose perspective. This is a theme I will pick up on later in this book when I describe my time working with police helicopters. You can never see the full picture, or make the best decisions, if you are only looking in one direction – usually at where the loudest noise or biggest drama is taking place. Sometimes you need to pull away and look at the full picture before making any conclusions.

If I could achieve just one thing as a result of writing a book about my life experiences, I hope that it is that people come away with an overall *positive* impression of the police. I feel as though we are living in an increasingly negative world and I want to do anything I can to help challenge that.

With the exception of one devastating and life-changing experience involving an abusive superior officer, which ultimately inspired me to embark on my new career and write this book, I had a positive experience working in the police service. I say police *service* and not police *force* on purpose. I always saw it as my duty to *serve* the public and assist them; force being used only as a last resort.

Since retiring from the police in 2020, I have invested my time in helping organisations revise their structure, especially in terms of the flow of communication from junior to senior levels. When I did encounter internal problems during my policing career, it was largely due to a breakdown in communication between different levels in the hierarchy. I believe there is much we can do to change our conduct and prevent this from happening.

INTRODUCTION

Throughout my career as a police officer, and since retiring, I've constantly been asked questions like, "What's it like being in the police?" and "What's the worst thing that's ever happened to you?" I've always jokingly said, "Where do I start; I could write a book." Finally, after much stopping and starting, I have done just that.

There are many books by police officers, but I do believe each one has something unique to offer. I wanted to write about my entire journey: into the police, through the police, and out of the police. None of it has been smooth sailing, but I don't have any regrets because all our experiences make us who we are, and I am happy with where I am today. I work closely with organisations to help them better understand complexity in their leadership structure and to discover and develop the full potential of innate talent in their people. There is certainly no "talent shortage", as is sometimes suggested by business "experts", it often simply lies undiscovered within organisations. I try to help managers locate and harness the talent in their teams, to tap into it instead of overlooking it.

I have always had a deep interest in people. I am particularly fascinated by what makes them sink or swim; what hinders them or helps them thrive. Why do bad things happen to good people? Why do inherently talented people sometimes fail? Why do some people get into roles they are unsuited for? Why do the wrong people so often get promoted and cause trickle-down problems in their chain of command? Why do some people become trapped within a role or career, always striving for promotion and success, driven mostly by status and salary rather than true job satisfaction?

We all have choices in life, and we all have lots of influences over us. When we make choices, we have to get the balance right between what we truly want and what those external influences are suggesting. I was lucky in that, early on in life, I had to challenge a very strong external influence. My mother did not want me to join the police. She was rightly worried about my safety and, knowing I have quite a sensitive disposition, was concerned about the effect the "bad stuff" would have on me. But I knew in my heart I dearly wanted to do it. In the end, she respected my choice. This is a good example of the importance of "speaking up" and "listening down". We must encourage children and young people to speak up and voice their internal feelings, to explore those subconscious ideas. Suppressing young voices will stifle innate talent that we so desperately need in the world. We must listen to young people and encourage them to share their thoughts and feelings.

By writing this book, I hope to kill two birds with one stone. First, I want to record my time in the police service so that the next time someone asks me "What was it like?" instead of saying, "I could write a book" I can say, "Here, it's all in my book"! But I am also trying to generate interest in, and provoke thought about, leadership. It is not only those at the top of an organisation who are leaders; those on the very bottom rung of the ladder need to be individual leaders, too. Leadership is not about being dictatorial, it is about serving others and showing compassion and understanding. Most of us will come across situations where we are required to lead at some points in our careers, no matter where we are positioned in an organisation.

Yes, there are times and occasions that require a formal command-and-control leadership style – when public order is essential, during a firearms incident, or at the scene of a major event – but the majority of decisions in the majority of situations do not need that type of authoritarian approach. We will always benefit from taking the time to obtain a greater understanding of the complexity of a situation and from collaborating with the people best suited to solving the problems. The best decisions usually come from having the greatest situational awareness. For this, we need self-awareness; we need to know exactly what attributes and preferences we innately possess, and how best to apply them in the right environments.

I didn't start off in life wanting to be a police officer. In fact, no one was more surprised than me when my career took this path. But once I was signed up, I knew it was the right line of work for me. For me, the "law enforcement" part of the job was always the "box-ticking" exercise. I was much more inspired by the part of the job that would put me in contact with people. That's what made me glad to get up in the morning and go to work… the knowledge that I could help make people's lives better.

Police work is often about dealing with the fallout when bad things happen to good people: damage control. It can be a thankless task. There are times when the public will really express their gratitude though – and often this will be in the most distressing circumstances. Those moments always make up for the bad times.

In my post-police career, I have been working in various capacities to help organisations improve their workplace environment by making it a psychologically healthier place where employees can thrive.

We start by ensuring that individuals have the opportunity to realise their own unique innate talents by using a process of self-exploration which results in self-awareness. Allowing people the space to speak for themselves, and about themselves, freely, without fearing judgement or negative repercussion is a key factor in reducing risk to any organisation. A high level of self-awareness can stop good people falling into the trap of trying to reach beyond their competence level, a trap that can so easily lead to ill health – with both mental and physical implications.

When we create more openness in the workplace, and foster a trusting environment, we give those at a more junior level the confidence to ask questions and give feedback from the front line, and we help those in more senior managerial positions stay attuned to the needs and experiences of their teams. All of this ensures that the essential synergy required for a healthy psychological environment is maintained. This in turn optimises the efficiency and creativity of the whole organisation.

Given the complexity of police work, I believe we need to work harder at understanding people in the organisation at large. I think we may have expected too much of our police officers in the past, expecting them all to be a "jack of all trades but master of none", and promoting people who are not best suited to positions of leadership. If we better understood our individual preferences and innate talents, I believe we could get the people into roles that best suit them. If we can improve our self-awareness, and get the right people doing the jobs they are best suited to, a thriving culture will naturally prevail. A healthy psychological environment would be a natural by-product of this process, rather than an objective that leaders chase and try to impose artificially.

PART ONE:

LEARNING:
A 30-YEAR POLICE CAREER

CHAPTER ONE:

NOT IN THE NAVY NOW

Unlike the majority of people, I did not come into this world alone; I had a travelling companion: my twin brother. Well, he'd remind me at this point that he did beat me to it by 14 minutes. So even though our sister is a full 8 years younger, I am jokingly known as the "middle child".

My brother and I were born in September 1967. There have been pros and cons to having a twin brother, but overall, I would say there are more "pros". We've always had each other to lean on, and fortunately we get on very well, so it's been like having a friend for life. Our parents tell us that we devised our very own language whilst playing together in our playpen. We were, and still are, inseparable, and have always shared many interests, such as our love of playing sport – particularly cricket, football, golf and tennis. Having always had similar skill levels in those sports, we've maintained a healthy rivalry throughout our lives. These days this comes out particularly when we are playing golf! We do have one weird "twin nuance", which is that while I play football right-footed but cricket left-handed, my twin brother is the mirror image of me playing football left-footed and cricket right-handed!

Music is another shared love. When we were 10 years old, my brother decided to play the euphonium whilst I chose the cornet. We went on to play in our school bands and local brass bands. I will somewhat begrudgingly admit that he had the greater talent for music. I am sure that if he had wanted, and had committed himself, he would have gone on to be one of the top euphonium players in the country. He was certainly more extrovert than me, and enjoyed solo performances and being the focus of attention on stage. At one point he was taken under the tutorship of Steven Mead, a Professor of Euphonium, and played for "the" top brass band of its day, Desford Colliery Dowty Band.

When people ask me what it is like to be a twin, I always say I don't know as I have always been a twin and actually will never know any different.

That I ended up joining the police was as much a surprise to me as it was to my family. Many of us grow up with a "dream job" in mind and mine was to be a helicopter pilot. I had a vision of landing a Westland Lynx on the back of a Royal Navy frigate in treacherous seas. I imagined battling the elements and gripping the controls as I fought to land the helicopter on the bucking deck of the ship as it was tossed about in the waves, bringing this powerful machine and the crew it was carrying back to safety. Some kids grow up wanting to be pilots because they want to fly big aircraft and travel the world doing it, but for me helicopters were so much more exciting. Being able to land anywhere and simply to hover in one spot held much more appeal. (Although I went on to discover that hovering in one spot really isn't that simple!)

I'm not sure when my desire to fly first started but I definitely caught some of the love from my father. Growing up, I remember how he would run out into the garden whenever an aircraft of any sort flew over. He would then attempt to name the manufacturer of it, his excitement escalating if it was a military aircraft or helicopter. We lived on the flight path into East Midlands airport so you can imagine my mother's exasperation at having her husband disappear at the faintest distant sound of an aircraft engine in the middle of meals and conversations. She would roll her brown eyes every time he rushed outside to watch them fly over our modest dormer bungalow in Burton upon Trent.

My determination to learn to fly was cemented when The Fleet Air Arm pitched up at my school in an immaculate grey Westland Lynx as part of their recruitment drive. I will never forget watching this incredible machine landing on the school's upper site sports field. I was mesmerised as I witnessed the crew shutting down the powerful engines, alighting in their flying overalls, bedecked with squadron badges and cool flying helmets. In that moment, I knew with absolute certainty that I wanted to be a helicopter pilot. It was the only time I felt hugely jealous of the head boy as he and the head girl were taken on a short flight over the rooftops of Burton. I thought it particularly unfair. I should have been allowed to go as I actually *wanted* to be a helicopter pilot. But as every child eventually learns: life is not "fair". You don't always get what you want, or even deserve. I learnt this lesson many times as a child; good practice for surviving a lot of "unfairness" in my police years.

My first big stumbling block came when I tried to apply to get into the Navy and found I couldn't complete the application form. One question became my undoing. It asked, "Have you ever had asthma in the past five years?" I half wish I'd lied now, but I know I wouldn't have been able to live with myself if I'd been found out. I believe you are nothing without your integrity. If you put that on the line, you have broken trust not only with others, but also – and more importantly – with yourself. It's very hard to regain that trust. When you go against your integrity, you only have everything to lose. If I'd lied and had then been found out, it would have ended my career in a disgraceful way. I couldn't risk that.

The one asthma attack I'd had, that happened to be within that previous five-year period, was during a 1500-metre running race. For once I was doing rather well on the grass track on the school sports field, despite the fact it was a sweltering summer's day. Eventually, I was in second position with only one lap left to run. I remember willing myself to win, imagining raising my hands in triumph over my head as I crossed the finish line, like my athletic heroes at that time, Steve Ovett and Sebastian Coe. But all of a sudden, I began to struggle for breath. I panicked. I felt as if I didn't know where my next breath was going to come from. I was terrified and had to stop running. Finally, I recovered my breathing, but I was completely out of the race, and crying from the sheer panic and shock. The sports teacher consoled me and advised me to see my GP, who prescribed me some pills to carry with me at all times and to take if I ever experienced a similar attack.

I have never had another asthma attack and now wonder if that one event wasn't simply a combination of me pushing myself and overheating in such hot weather. But when I was filling out that application form, all I could think was: if I lie on the form and have another attack, or they ask for my medical records, I could lose everything. So, I decided to put my application on hold for at least five years, hoping I would then be able to answer truthfully that I hadn't had an asthma attack in the five preceding years.

This was a difficult decision, but I have never regretted it. There have been many times in my life when I've needed to remind myself that your integrity is everything. It is the one thing no one can take from you, and that, even when it comes to making a difficult decision, or losing out on something, there is nothing worth making a serious compromise in your integrity for.

Frustrated and dejected, I tried to think of what I should do with my life in the intervening time. My twin brother had left school during the first year of sixth form to become a trainee architectural technician. My father had trained as a draftsman after leaving school and had worked his way up to becoming a well-respected contracts manager for Conder – a local company that manufactured steel-framed buildings, so this was an industry we were familiar with.

I, myself, had done a week's work experience in the "buildings" office of Ind Coope Brewery. Along with Marston's and Bass, Ind Coope Brewery was one of the huge breweries situated in Burton, which had made it the brewing capital of the UK. Being such a large company, Ind Coope had its own construction and engineering services department, which included architects, structural engineers and quantity surveyors. During my week's work experience, I had been introduced to the world of quantity surveying. I discovered that it was more than simply "counting bricks", that it included providing estimations and feasibility studies, and involved conducting financial and contractual negotiations between builders and clients. It appeared to be quite a varied and interesting career. It certainly wasn't flying helicopters, but I found it quite interesting.

As a result of these factors, it was a natural progression for me to decide to get qualified as a quantity surveyor.

My A' level results were just about good enough to get me a place, through the "clearing system" (when they offer places that they can't fill to people with grades below those normally required) on a 4-year Quantity Surveying course at the Polytechnic of Wales at Pontypridd. By chance, my dad had to travel to nearby Merthyr Tydfil for work and so offered to take me down to have a look at the polytechnic and even start searching for somewhere to live during the course.

The visit was not a success. For starters, the weather was particularly grim and did nothing to enhance the town of Pontypridd; the greyness making the hilly mining community look particularly bleak, uninspiring and uninviting. When I arrived at the university, the sour-faced lecturer who greeted me for my welcome interview, sifted through his papers, found my A' level results and remarked, bluntly, "I didn't think we were letting people in with grades that low!"

A short chat with him tipped me over the edge. I met my dad back at his car and told him I wasn't taking up my place. I was so resolute, I even refused to go and look for lodgings, much to his disappointment. My mother was even more devastated by my decision. She hadn't had the opportunity of higher education even though she'd dearly wanted to, and I think she wanted to achieve her ambitions through me. I didn't like disappointing my mother, but I knew it wasn't the right thing for me, and I am grateful my parents didn't force me in the way many parents force their children to go in a certain direction or take up opportunities they hadn't had themselves.

I have never regretted this particular decision.

However, without any new ideas about what to do, it seemed quantity surveying was still destined to be my path into employment and my dad helped find me a job as a trainee in a very reputable company called Gleeds. They were based in Nottingham but had an office in Burton. I was much happier with the idea of continuing to live at home for a while, and the fact that I would earn a small wage. My mother was consoled by the fact that, as part of the apprenticeship, I would be attending Trent Polytechnic in Nottingham once a week, and that I would eventually get a degree.

Alas, her dreams were destined to be dashed again!

I did, however, last three years at Gleeds. Their satellite office in Burton had been set up to obtain work from the numerous local breweries, such as Bass, Marston's and Ind Coope, that were dotted around the area. The office was on the top floor of a building called "Peel House" as it had once been owned by the family of Robert Peel, who founded the Metropolitan Police Service – perhaps a foreshadowing of my future life. I loved it firstly because it overlooked Peel Croft, the home of Burton RFC, but more importantly because it was only 15 minutes from home and meant that I could still play for the local cricket team and play cornet in the brass band (coincidentally, sponsored by Ind Coope). I dutifully paid my parents a small amount of my pay packet for "board and lodgings."

I soon discovered quantity surveying was not for me. I was bored. I identified with the joke I once heard about working in quantity surveying, "Don't look out of the window in the morning as you'll have nothing to do in the afternoon." It was only the nature of the work I didn't like; the people I worked with were great. I got involved with team activities, even running a half marathon with a colleague, and visited some amazing parts of the country. I also became a "real" beer drinker rather than a lager lout! There were frequent visits to the Ruddles Brewery in Oakham, Rutlandshire. But these were all brief highlights. I wasn't happy. I didn't feel I was fulfilling any purpose.

From the window in my office (which I did look out of much more than once a day), I had a great view of busy Lichfield Street. I would watch the traffic go by and see people making their way in and out of the nearby town centre. I would regularly see police officers walking around in their smart blue uniforms, long trench coats and large helmets displaying the force crest. Sometimes they would be walking alone, sometimes they were in pairs. Sometimes I would see them speeding past in their brightly painted yellow "budgie" police cars (an early attempt at a multi coloured police car, quite avant-garde in the late 1980s). They would speed past with sirens blazing and the single "flowerpot" blue light flashing away on the roof. I would find myself curiously wondering where they might be going. And what would they find when they got there? Were they chasing a stolen car? Had there been a burglary? I became quite envious of them. How incredible, I thought, to be able to turn up for work each day with no idea what you might face, going somewhere not knowing what you might find there, having the possibility of being able to make a significant difference to someone's life in some way. Very soon I realised this was my destiny. I could see my purpose. I was going to join the police service.

My mother was not happy. She tried to warn me off. "You won't like it. It's dangerous. You'll see some horrible things. You'll have to go to car accidents and post-mortems and see dead bodies. You'll meet some evil people." She was right on every count. I saw some terrible things I can never unsee. However, the most egregious example of evil I ever encountered sadly came from within the police service itself, not from out on the streets.

Seeing she was failing to talk me out of it, my mother recruited my elderly and staunchly Methodist grandmother, whose best attempt at dissuading me was to warn me that the wearing of a helmet would "spoil" my "curls"! But I was prepared to have flattened curls if I could make a positive difference to many people. I knew it was my destiny. I was excited about it. To appease my elderly grandmother, I told a little white lie and assured her that if I did eventually manage to join the police, I would probably be given clerical duties and would not have to go outside and face the unpredictable public. She seemed reassured by this for a while. And much later on in my career, when I briefly trained as a firearms officer, I hid the fact from her and my mother. What they didn't know wouldn't hurt them.

When my mother realised that neither she nor my grandmother were putting me off my determined decision, she made me promise that I would speak to friends and acquaintances who were in the police force to get a better perspective of what I would be getting myself into. Several of the cricket team I played with were police officers and I sat down with the club captain, who happened to be a detective at Burton. He outlined all the pros and cons and then I asked him a final question.

"If you had your time again, would you join the police again?"

He answered without hesitation: "No". He explained how much had changed, in his opinion for the worse, since he had joined some 25 years ago. In his opinion, the 1984 Police and Criminal Evidence Act had stopped "real" criminals being removed from the streets.

These days, I'm the experienced former police officer that young people thinking of joining the police ask for advice. If ever asked I refuse to commit to an answer to the question I asked my old cricket club captain, because I think everyone needs to make their own mind up based on the facts, and not on the emotional response of someone who is probably jaded and a bit of an anachronism! I wouldn't want to put anyone off from what is an amazing and fulfilling occupation in so many ways. It is obviously going to be a mixed bag of experiences. And the police service goes through changes all the time, so it can never be the same for someone just joining today as it once was for someone on their way out. Ultimately, though, I know that there isn't much point in answering the question because it would not put someone off; just as nothing put me off. I joined despite all the voices telling me not to.

*

It's never a bad idea to be challenged. In his book, *The Barcelona Way: Unlocking the DNA of a Winning Culture*, Damian Hughes explains how those irritating people (you know the sort, you find them in every organisation) who put up objections or resistance to ideas and change, are actually serving a very real and important purpose. They appear negative and seem to undermine every amazing and innovative idea that you conjure up, but they could be saving you from making mistakes because they unwittingly stress test your idea for its strengths and weaknesses. It's easy to see your precious idea through rose-tinted glasses. It's important to be challenged, to be made to probe deeper, questioning things you might not have thought of. You might be saved from falling flat on your face at the first hurdle. You should be grateful to have people forcing you to examine your ideas from angles you may not have thought of.

There is a concept, rumoured to have been devised by the Israeli intelligence service, Mossad, called the "10th Man" – or the "devil's advocate exercise". I like to refer to it, more generally, as being the "contrarian mind" in any given situation. The idea is that, wherever you have a group of 10 people trying to deal with a problem or make a decision, and 9 of them are in direct agreement with one another, it becomes the duty of the "10th Man" to provide a contrarian opinion and voice. This ensures that no possibility or hypothetical eventuality is overlooked, no matter how extreme or unlikely it may be. It allows people to take a step back, to think critically, and to explore all potential problems and alternative solutions, ensuring nothing is overlooked. I would argue that we all need to think more critically in most situations, that we should all employ our own "contrarian mind" more often.

When it came to my making a decision about joining the police, my mother became my "10th man" and acted as my "contrarian mind". She made me stop and think, and question aspects of policing I hadn't considered before. She helped me realise that I wasn't just looking at a police career in an idealistic way, it was definitely what I really wanted to do.

I will never forget posting the application off. I remember the moment vividly. I had just finished rehearsals with the brass band I played in. It was a Friday night and we were off to the curry house. The post office was on the way, on New Street opposite the old Victorian fire station. I remember dropping the A4 brown envelope into the post box, which was a hole in the wall. I remember the moment it left my fingers and the sound it made when it hit the bottom of the post box. I felt this seal of my fate; I knew there was no way back, that I had embarked upon the journey of becoming a police officer and all the adventures that it would ultimately bring.

I took and passed the police exam in April 1988 and was invited to an interview and physical test. On 14th February 1989, I was asked to complete a one and a half mile run around the streets that circled the Cannock Road headquarters on the outskirts of Stafford. I always wondered what the local residents thought as they watched the hundreds of would-be police officers pounding the pavements of their neighbourhood. Did they speculate, as they watched people run or stagger depending on fitness level, on who would pass or fail the test?

I passed the fitness test and went on to the interview stage. I recall two particular questions put to me by the rather rigid looking, tunic-clad senior officers conducting the interview. The first was, "What newspaper do you read?" and the other was, "What rank do you see yourself reaching in your career?"

I could rarely be bothered to read the newspaper but when I did it was the *Daily Mail*, as that was what my parents bought. I wanted to seem a little more intellectual and well-read than I was, so I answered, "Either *The Times* or *The Guardian*."

As for the rank, again I sought to give the answer that they wanted to hear rather than actually ask myself what I wanted. I didn't want to seem overly ambitious by saying, "Chief Constable" but I also didn't want to come across as an underachiever by saying, "Sergeant", so I said, "Superintendent."

A Chief Constable is the highest-ranking officer within any police service apart from The Met (Metropolitan Police Service) in London, which has a "Commissioner" in place of a "Chief Constable", making that position the highest ranking in the country. A Superintendent is four ranks below a Chief Constable and a very senior role, one that usually leads several hundreds of officers across a division or department. And it is about four ranks above the entry-level rank of a qualified police officer – i.e. that of Constable, so it seemed about the right one to state. In the end, I discovered that the rank of Sergeant, which is just one rank above a Constable and three ranks below Superintendent, suited me perfectly; I came to feel like I'd found the best job in the world.

*

When you retire from the police, you are entitled to look through your personal records. I chose to do this out of curiosity. After wading through the dossier stretching back over the 30 years that I'd spent as a police officer, I found some of the observations made by the superintendent (whose name was redacted in black marker pen) at my interview. His final comment was:

"A smart, intelligent and articulate young man. Appears to have thought through his application quite carefully. Does not appear very robust despite his sporting interests. Provided that he can cope with the physical side of the service, he should go a long way." That was a good prediction, seeing as my career took me as far as Jamaica!

After the interview, I had a tense few weeks waiting to find out how I'd fared. I constantly feared the worst, as we are all prone to do when we passionately want something. Finally, at the beginning of April, an official-looking brown Manila envelope eventually dropped through our letterbox. It contained a letter signed by the then Chief Constable, Charles Kelly, inviting me to begin my training as a police officer. I was in. The journey had begun.

The next hurdle was telling my parents. My dad wasn't one to show much emotion, but I think he was proud of me. Perhaps he felt a twinge of good-natured jealousy, too, as I suspect he would have liked to have joined the police rather than being cajoled into becoming a draughtsman. He continually informs me that he was the best police officer Staffordshire Police never had! My mother was somewhat muted in her response. I'm sure she would have been happier if I'd remained in my nice "safe" job, sat behind a desk, and had continued with my studies at the polytechnic. I think she secretly hoped I wouldn't last the course.

I know my parents both wanted the best for me, and they ultimately supported my choices, but my mother definitely would have preferred what *she* thought was best for me. I think many parents want to live their lives again, vicariously, through their children, possibly because they didn't achieve everything they wanted in their lives and they see their children as a chance to have "another go", but every person has to live their own life and forge their own path. You can't live your life for someone else or you'll never fulfil your unique purpose and reach your full potential. Far too many people simply plough a furrow straight through the field of life because it seems like the easiest thing to do. They never stop to wonder what might be over yonder, or peer over the hedge into the adjacent field to explore what riches lie there. Ultimately, I wanted to follow my dream and still make my parents proud of me, in my own way.

There was one final hoop to jump through before I could start my training: a "home visit" by a sergeant from the local police station who came over to our house to speak to me and my parents one evening. I struggled to keep a straight face as I introduced Sergeant Sergeant (his actual name) to my parents. For a fleeting moment I wandered if my mother, scared as she was about me joining the police, might try to sabotage the visit by putting on some act like perhaps staggering around with a large glass of gin pretending to be drunk and swearing profusely, in the hope that Sergeant Sergeant might report that the offer should be withdrawn as I clearly came from a disreputable and unstable home. But no, she behaved impeccably. I was touched by her support.

And that was it, I was in. I couldn't wait to report for training.

Northamptonshire "spiky"-topped helmets. Unfortunately, I had forgotten to lock my bedroom door and that's how I had my first encounter with the larger-than-life character and relentless practical joker, Mark Mould. Mark burst into my room, caught me in my helmet and shouted out, "We've got another one here!" and the rest of the lads piled in to laugh at me admiring myself in my new kit. I remembered then that someone once said to me, "If you can't take a joke, don't join the police!"

I later witnessed Mark's less-than-amusing experience in the police boxing championships. This was an annual event held in Stafford. All new recruits were expected to take part during their two-year probationary period. Fortunately, I got knocked out in the first training session – literally. I hadn't been well since a trip abroad and, after being subjected to a high-impact training regime I'd never before experienced, finally collapsed and hit the floor. I was taken to the North Staffordshire Royal Infirmary for a cursory check-up and the doctor there signed me off any more training, so I avoided being beaten to a pulp in a boxing ring!

Mark didn't get so lucky.

I vividly remember walking into the venue and feeling uncomfortable as I saw the set-up that was reminiscent of what I imagine gladiator events might have looked like. The boxing ring was centre stage with a raised platform to one side: here sat all the high-ranking police officers – including the chief constable himself – and their entourage. They looked like Caesar and his sycophants as they strode in and took their places, watching as the minions (trainees) beat each other to a pulp... getting the thumbs up or thumbs down from Caesar depending on whether he was pleased or not.

Mark was fighting in the super heavyweight section. The bouts were just two rounds and Mark managed the first round but then took a full-on blow to his nose. I had never seen so much blood. The award he received for "Bravest Boxer" was meagre compensation for the two weeks he spent in hospital while they rebuilt his broken nose. You do have to wonder what rationale goes into risking the loss of a good police officer for two weeks simply in the name of providing some rather barbaric entertainment for the pleasure of the Chief Constable. That was the first and last police boxing match I ever attended.

The sight of so much blood gushing out of Mark's nose was not something I'd prepared for. Unlike my anticipated first trip to a post mortem. My mother's voice echoing in my head: "You won't like it!" I sat, nervously, in the minibus with my fellow recruits, on the day that – as part of our first module – we were transported to the North Staffordshire Royal Infirmary to witness our first post mortem. We'd heard the horror stories, in particular about the smell. The advice was to put some of that menthol-eucalyptus chest vapour rub for coughs on a handkerchief and hold it to your nose. I dreaded the moment we might be told we had to watch a body being dissected. I thought I'd never get through it without passing out. We all purchased copious amounts of extra-strong mints, too.

However, we were to be pleasantly disappointed. The green-gowned mortician who greeted us informed us that, sadly, there were no bodies there that day.

I for one, let out a huge sigh of relief.

Obviously, I was not spared the sight of dead bodies for long. Throughout the duration of my career, I saw many.

And it never got any easier. This led me to make a very interesting observation. I slowly came to conclude that there are two types of people in the police – and perhaps in life. There are those who are squeamish about blood and gore, but they also tend to be the ones who are good at delivering bad news to relatives or holding the hands of survivors at the side of the road after a particularly bad traffic accident. They are the more compassionate and empathetic type. Then there are those who are able to pick up severed body parts without even seeming to flinch, yet the idea of sitting with a person and talking gently to them, consoling them, would be a real challenge. They are the most dissociated type. Neither is "better" or more valuable than the other. We need both. We need a diverse range of skills and qualities in all organisations.

The initial four weeks of training at our headquarters flashed by and the twelve of us became a tight-knit unit. We learnt how to take orders, keep our kit clean and pressed, and even attempted a little marching. The next stage of our training was to be a 10-week stint at the regional training school at Ryton-on-Dunsmore, near Coventry.

The regional training centre catered for new recruits from all of the Midlands police forces, including Derbyshire, West Midlands, Nottinghamshire, Northamptonshire, Warwickshire and Leicestershire and to make the groups more diverse, our close group of twelve Staffordshire Officers was to be split up and there ended up being about three of us in each of the 'inter-force' groups.

We soon bonded and found the local pub where we could relax after the daily routine of learning about legal procedures, doing more ironing, a little marching and plenty of physical exercise. I was eating three very substantial meals a day (more than I would have eaten at home) but wasn't gaining any weight as I was burning it all off. We played a lot of football and even managed to beat the instructors in a not-so-friendly match. I was quickly discovering that police officers can be exceptionally competitive. I heard stories of many inter-divisional or inter-force sporting event that had ended in an unsavoury exchange of words, or even fists! And I heard rumours that some recruits were selected primarily for their sporting prowess as many chief constables coveted the national trophies handed out for football, rugby and cricket. At times I wondered whether my considerable cricketing experience had gone some way towards helping me with my initial selection.

The majority of new recruits I met at Ryton came from the West Midlands as they were by far the biggest metropolitan force in the Midlands. I learned that they had recently increased the maximum joining age to 45 years and one in our midst had just made it under the wire. This man was a lanky and lofty (standing at 6'7" tall) ex-miner. He had actually been a Staffordshire coal miner since leaving school and I was in awe of the life he'd lived underground at the coal face. He showed us the multitude of small black lines across the backs of his hands, explaining that they were cuts he'd received whilst working with the coal. The cuts had become filled with fine coal dust and the result was like a web of fine threads all over his skin. I'll never forget the night he almost missed our strict 9.30pm curfew to be signed back in after a night at the pub. In order to make it, he made a shortcut across the manicured lawn in front of the reception: a route that was strictly forbidden. He was sent to the commandant for a gruff dressing down for this misdemeanour. I remember thinking how strange it was that a man who'd spent almost 30 years in the toughest conditions could get a ticking off for running across a piece of grass.

It was at Ryton where I experienced, first hand, the peculiar and unique culture of the police force. There was so much to take in and it included the history, the uniform, the traditions, the discipline, the rules and many nuances.

One peculiarity that I noticed early on, one that made me uneasy, was the inability of some of the staff and recruits to connect on a human level. I used to walk, with one of my friends, to the on-site canteen for breakfast and we would try to say hello to anyone who walked past us in the opposite direction. Our efforts at being friendly and jovial were in vain. Almost exclusively, people would ignore us, and even avoid us as they became aware that we were about to wish them a good morning. I couldn't believe that people in the same organisation couldn't spare a moment to wish another raw recruit a good morning in return. If they weren't prepared to say hello to a fellow recruit, how were they going to behave with members of the public?

I soon noticed that the worst offenders for this avoidant behaviour were those from the West Midlands Police. This puzzled me until I discovered that they had recently gone through a very large recruitment drive and had found themselves with a majority of ex-service personnel. Perhaps there was a culture clash, or a feeling of superiority amongst these recruits with their military background, who looked down on those of us who they regarded as being less experienced than them. Either way, I really felt the coldness and wished I could do something about it.

Some 30 years later, I happened to be back at Staffordshire Police headquarters – running a training course – and I witnessed exactly the same behaviour. The only difference being that people now had mobile phones they could bury their heads in to make it even easier to avoid making any connection. There was even a rumour that a very senior officer had been witnessed holding his phone up to his ear, pretending to be on a call as he walked past someone he didn't wish to acknowledge, only for the phone to start ringing suddenly, rumbling his ruse!

I wished I could do something to help people connect with each other. I even thought of a scheme called a "HAY" zone, which would stand for a "How Are You?" Zone and contemplated setting up signposts at either end of a walkway so that people could be encouraged to say hello to each other as they passed through that particular stretch. I never did that (I'm sure the disappointment of people giving that a wide berth would have been even more depressing) but if you know an environment that could benefit from this, give it a go. Nothing will change unless we actively try to make those changes.

The foundation course went well and we "passed out" just before Christmas 1989. My parents came to see the event and I think they were both very proud of their son marching to the police band wearing his pristine uniform and ceremonial white gloves.

The senior officer, taking the salute, was the Chief Constable of the West Midlands Police, Geoffrey Dear, who became quite a controversial figure over the years, for leading the investigation into the Hillsborough Stadium disaster and being in charge when the notorious West Midlands

Serious Crime Squad was in its last throes. These days he sits in the House of Lords as Baron Dear, a crossbench peer. An imposing figure, standing at well over six-foot tall, he dwarfed the majority of the nervous recruits as he inspected the lines of tunic-clad officers. Only our 6'7" Staffordshire ex-miner saw eye to eye with him.

Geoffrey Dear was the first person who I felt had a specific aura about him, a presence that you couldn't help but be in awe of. He gave the keynote speech at the passing out ball, held at the headquarters, during which he mentioned that one of the highlights of his career was having Wolverhampton twinned with Beirut. To this day I'm not sure if this was true!

A highlight of the evening was watching all the senior officers parade up to their top table, resplendent in uniforms I'd never ever seen before. They looked as if they'd stolen my mother's curtain's gold braid swags and tails and had them sewn onto their jackets.

The event was a wonderful way to celebrate the start of our careers and say goodbye to some of the friends we'd made who were from different forces. It was quite sad to think we wouldn't ever be working together as that tight unit again. But we were all looking forward to some well-deserved time off for Christmas before the final stage of our training, which was to spend five weeks with our tutors, after which we were expected to be ready for duty. The prospect was daunting to say the least, but it was also thrilling to think about kicking off our careers as fully trained police officers.

CHAPTER THREE:

STOKIES PAST AND PRESENT

I considered myself extremely fortunate to be assigned a tutor constable I got on so well with. Dave Malam was a real larger-than-life character with a heart of gold and the patience of a saint. We had some common interests, including football, and shared a light-hearted sense of humour. He was a level-headed, "no nonsense" copper who had worked with people from all walks of life, and of all ages and ethnicities, so he could fit in with anyone. He could read situations quickly and make good judgement calls. He was the perfect role model to learn from and be guided through the period of tutorship by, and he remained someone I could go to for advice in the early stages of my career.

Dave's passion was Stoke City FC, which was, at that time, a second division club. In fact, he was so well informed and had so many opinions about them, I sometimes suspected he was secretly managing them on the side! Dave always seemed to find himself standing on "sentry duty" at the entrance to the tunnel. (Police officers are positioned by the tunnel that the players and officials use, and which is situated at the half-way line, between dug-outs of the home and away teams.) In this position, he would be responsible for protecting both the players and staff from any errant or overzealous fans that might try to get too close and would also be on hand to calm things down if managers became too aggressive towards each other, or the referee. Dave loved being in the heat of the action whenever Stoke City played a home game; he was able to hear what was being said by managers of both sides as they deliberated match tactics with their respective players and team officials and brought this into his actual legitimate role as manager of our Stoke Police Division team, which he ran as if it was indeed Stoke City FC!

Football was a real bonding ground for me. I loved it and was able to play to a reasonably good standard. I was once even described by my school sports teacher as a "cultured right-back" after we won the U16 School's Staffordshire Cup, by which I think he meant that I was a good safe bet, a consistent defender, reliably always where I was supposed to be. Football was definitely a real asset in the process of getting to know my new colleagues and gaining some respect.

A real highlight of my time serving in Stoke was the occasion I got to play at the Victoria Ground (home of Stoke City FC) in the final of the local "Haig and Haig" Cup (named after its Whiskey-producing sponsor). The league was played on a Thursday afternoon and was known as the "Half-holiday League" and included other divisional police sides as well as teams from the fire service and NHS. Of course, it was an extremely proud moment for Dave. For once, he wasn't on duty at the entrance to the tunnel, he was actually in pride of place in the manager's dug-out. He sat there looking like all his Christmases had come at once! He relished the moment; he'd even hung up all the players' kit in the changing rooms as if we were professionals.

Playing to a crowd of about 50 in a stadium designed to hold 56,000 was slightly surreal but made it no less thrilling to be playing on the pitch where some of the footballing greats, including the legendary Sir Stanley Matthews, had played. It was exhausting playing on a full-size pitch, though. I had never appreciated quite how huge it would feel compared to how it looks from the stands. I wasn't sorry to be substituted during the second half; I was absolutely shattered. We unfortunately lost the game but that didn't spoil our enjoyment of the experience, which included using the luxury bath in the changing rooms that seemed to be about half the size of an Olympic swimming pool!

This once-in-a-lifetime experience was matched only by the excitement of meeting the great Sir Stanley Matthews himself... thanks to my tutor! Dave had become something of a self-appointed security guard to Sir Stanley, who had moved back to Stoke in his latter years, buying a beautiful home in Penkhull, Stoke-on-Trent, overlooking the Victoria Ground. Of course, he still travelled regularly and spent long periods of time abroad on coaching assignments. Dave would regularly check up on the house, which was up a steep road and tucked away around a corner. On one occasion we arrived at the property to check on it and there was a car parked in the driveway and the front door was wide open. Somewhat concerned, we parked up ourselves and went to investigate. As we approached the front door, a small, elderly, grey-haired figure appeared from the shadows. I recognised him almost immediately and couldn't believe I was staring at the legend himself. Sir Stanley invited us in for a cup of tea and we had a wonderful chat. He was warm, humorous and animated; I was quite star-struck. I remembered his kind face when I read his autobiography, *The Way it Was*. He was an extremely benevolent man who gave much time and money to worthy causes. His passion for football knew no bounds and he particularly loved coaching children in lower income communities in South Africa and the USA. For all his fame and fortune, I had witnessed what a truly down-to-earth and genuinely generous man he was.

Stoke itself was a great place to cut my teeth as a police officer. The city of Stoke-on-Trent is actually made up of six towns. Stoke is just one of them, the other five being: Burslem, Tunstall, Fenton, Hanley and Longton. The smallish town of Stoke had limited nightlife with the main nightclubs in the area being in either Hanley or Newcastle Under Lyme, but we did attract a high degree of crime, some of it coming from the local area, but also an influx from Birmingham and Merseyside. There were some big, salubrious homes that attracted burglars in Trentham, which is an area on the outskirts of Stoke-on-Trent, just off the M6 motorway – ideal for fast getaways. There were also the industrial sites at Fenton with several warehouses packed with all sorts of products to tempt local petty thieves. These warehouses stored anything from fine bone china produced at the local potteries to shelves of toilet rolls that sat in the large "cash-and-carry" warehouses: people will steal anything they can use or sell!

So, we weren't just involved with public order, we had

real opportunities to stop crime, particularly on the night shifts. We also covered one of the busiest magistrates' courts in England at the time, which was based in Fenton, and we had one of the very first Accident and Emergency Trauma Centres at the North Staffs Royal Infirmary in Hartshill. Our shifts were never dull, but we weren't overwhelmed to the point of drowning in paperwork, which we knew happened in other areas of the country. And I was very happy, with enough variety in my days to keep me engaged and allow me to feel that I was making a difference in a few people's lives.

The French criminologist, Dr Edmond Locard (1877—1966), known as the "Sherlock Holmes of France" developed the basic principle of forensic science, "Every contact leaves a trace", which became known as "Locard's exchange". He meant this in the context of forensic detective work – for example, fingerprints and clothing fibres, but I believe it is also true of people we come into contact with in our everyday lives.

Everyone we meet, no matter whether for a fleeting moment or a lifelong relationship, leaves an impression on us, a trace or a mark. It might be good or bad, pleasant or unpleasant, memorable or forgettable, but it affects us, even in the smallest way.

I started my two-year probationary period with a real zest for the job. And I felt immediately in good company and good hands. I got along with everyone on my shift and our superiors. We were kept in line by the laid-back, chain-smoking Inspector Pete Lightfoot. An invitation into his office during the early hours of a night shift would involve the challenge of trying to make out his face through a cloud of thick smoke created by a combination of roll-ups and B&H cigarettes. How I don't miss the days of smoking being permissible in offices! Our custody sergeant, Sgt Pete Aston, was a worldly-wise chap, and completing the trio of our supervisory officers was the rather gruff Sgt Bill Fairclough, who was the shift's patrol sergeant and managed all the incidents we attended. There was a healthy balance of youth and experience across the team. Some of us young bucks needed more guidance than others. There were some of us who were approaching our new careers with some trepidation and then there were those who were just desperate to get out there and "lock up the baddies". According to these lads, if you hadn't arrested at least one person each night, whilst working a set of seven nights in a shift, you really weren't pulling your weight!

When I joined the police, officers worked three different shifts on a four-weekly continuous roster. There were the "earlies" which were 6am until 2pm, "noons" which were 2pm until 10pm and "nights" which filled in that period of 10pm until 6am the following day. In every four-week period, you were rostered on to work a stretch of seven nights with the remaining three weeks being made up of a combination of earlies and noons. What really hit me, in terms of fatigue, was the dreaded "quick changeover", which generally occurred twice every four weeks. This was when we finished a "noon" shift at 10pm and then had to return the following day for an early shift with only 8 hours respite between the two shifts, less if we'd had to work overtime on the previous night shift.

The most dreaded call when we were on "earlies", which was particularly common on Sunday mornings, was being asked to attend a "Form 12". This meant a sudden death in the home and involved the upsetting experience of dealing with people – the relatives or people who lived with the deceased – at their lowest point, full of emotion and grief. There was also the grim task of checking the body for any unusual marks that might have raised suspicions over the cause of death. There was one aspect of this task I never minded doing, however, and that was taking the statement that covered the deceased's life. This was usually a long process, but it always fascinated me, and I couldn't help but think about the strange juxtaposition of me sitting there, writing down all these vibrant and colourful details about someone's life whilst their body was lying upstairs getting cold, waiting for the undertakers to come and take it away. I also expanded my knowledge of the local history in this rather macabre way because many of the people I had to document worked in the local pottery industry, or "down the pit". This aspect of policing – being with people at what is often the lowest moment of their lives and offering comfort, occasionally even a shoulder to cry on – is not as widely publicised as the other more obvious and traditional aspects of policing.

Another frequent call out on "earlies", although somewhat less traumatic, were "Doulton Breaks". I kept hearing about this phenomenon during my training and eventually discovered the meaning. Many workers in the pottery industry would spend years saving up to purchase one of the prized porcelain figurines from Royal Doulton Pottery. They would then proudly display these figures – such as the Balloon Lady, Top O'The Hill or Ninette – on the front window sills of their terraced homes. These workers often had a hard life and their prized possession would bring a little joy to their lives. Burglars would scope out these households and then do a "smash and grab" in the night. Sadly, there was a good worldwide market for these stolen pieces, and they would attract good prices, so it was an easy haul for a casual burglar.

What particularly upset me when I saw someone's prized possession stolen in such a violent manner was that many of these people were coming up against particularly hard times. All the communities in and around Stoke were hard hit by the closures of the coal mines and pottery factories. It became an increasingly deprived area as unemployment sky-rocketed. The people were very proud, too, which led to a lot of social tension. I was more than aware of these factors as I started policing this area; I knew I had to stay sensitive to what these people were being put through.

At that time, the probationary period was two years; these days it's gone up to three. As long as we were probationers, we would get the tasks that no one else wanted. Owing to the fact I was a probationer, and Stoke's public mortuary being located within the boundaries of our subdivision, I found myself with a particularly onerous task in those early days of my career. Basically, any person dying overnight anywhere in the Stoke metropolitan area had to be housed in the mortuary. The keys were kept at the Stoke Police Station and, if someone died, the probationer on duty would be given the responsibility of getting the keys, opening up the front door of the mortuary, walking in and through the building to the back, where the cold storage was, to open the back doors for the unloading of the body. This was a discreet access point where ambulances and funeral directors' vehicles could unload and load bodies without being sighted by the unsuspecting public. The most gruesome part of the job was the "tagging". After a dead body had been unloaded by the ambulance crew and placed on a large tray, we had to take down the name of the deceased and other relevant information, and then write it down on what looked like a large luggage tag, which we then had to place around one of the toes on the body! Once this had been completed, we had to slide the body into the dark void behind the refrigerator's large silver door. If we were lucky, the funeral directors who had brought the deceased to the mortuary would assist us with the administration of the body. Then we would have to lock the door at the back, walk through the building and ensure the front door was locked again. I always remember thinking, when it was my turn to carry out this mortifying duty… who would ever break in to a place like this? I lost count of the number of times I had to carry out this unpleasant duty. I remember it was particularly unnerving when I had to do it alone. At least if I had a fellow probationer with me, we could fend off the spookiness with a bit of gallows humour!

The process of "bagging and tagging" the dead was usually quite a smooth one, with the exception of during one particular period when the ambulance drivers were on strike between 1989 and 1990. During this time, the job of transferring patients was given to the Army. Their regulation green Land Rovers were not equipped like ambulances and so the whole job was carried out in a very basic manner.

There was one particular night during the ambulance drivers' strike when I was radioed by the station's control room to get the keys and meet an Army vehicle at the back of the mortuary. To my absolute horror, as I arrived at the front of the mortuary, I saw that the Army vehicle was at the front door, with an ambulance that had been stationed there with necessary equipment. Two Army medics had already unloaded the dead body onto a stretcher and were waiting in full view of the pub opposite that was just beginning to empty out. I hastily advised the medics to reload the body into the Land Rover and drive around to the back door before too many prying eyes had gathered!

A key part of our training was to become skilled in administering first aid. This was often called upon in the line of duty, but there is one particular memory that is hard to shake.

I was on the early shift (6am until 2pm), which was usually a fairly quiet time. Our time on these shifts was generally spent picking up statements for the previous night's burglaries or thefts, or the odd sudden death, or interviewing suspects who'd been arrested during the night by the previous shift. On the morning in question, I was in the station helping out the front counter and control room when an excited young woman came bursting into the front reception, shouting, "He's having a heart attack! Come and help, quick!" She was distraught. She had sped the half mile from the scene on the busy A500 to the police station, pulled up haphazardly in Boothen Road, just outside the station, and then ran in shouting for help. Once I'd calmed her down enough to speak coherently, she explained that a man had stopped his car in the road in the middle of the morning commuter traffic and was clearly in a bad way.

There were no other patrols available for the job and so I jumped into a panda car, activated the blue lights and the siren – known as the "two tones" – and set off on the short journey to the huge traffic island (now replaced by a concrete flyovers and underpasses) that then existed at the junction where the A50 met the A500 – probably the busiest intersection in Stoke.

By the time I arrived at the spot where the stationary Ford Sierra Estate was located, a small crowd had gathered, though I immediately noted that no ambulance had arrived yet. Before leaving the station, I had checked with my control room that an ambulance was on its way, so I was reassured I wouldn't be there on my own for long.

One thing I was slowly getting used to during my probationary period was the expectations people have when they see a police officer in uniform. They can't know whether the officer has been on the job for three days or three years – when people see a uniformed officer, they expect that person to be able to take charge and know exactly what to do. The pressure is immense! On this occasion, as I approached the body of a large man lying on his back in the road, the people who'd been standing or kneeling around him cleared a path for me, and I soon found myself kneeling next to him thinking fast about what I should do.

I followed the protocols I'd learned, checking for a pulse or breath, and once I'd established the absence of either, I realised it was time to attempt mouth-to-mouth resuscitation. I found the protective covering we'd been issued for use in such an event and attempted to place it over the man's mouth. After a couple of hasty attempts, I realised it just wasn't working so I had no other choice but to do it the old-fashioned way; flesh on flesh. I ensured the man's tongue was out of the way, took a deep breath, pushed aside my queasy feelings and got on with giving this man mouth-to-mouth resuscitation. I kept it going for what seemed to be an eternity, conducting the 15 chest compressions to the two breaths. When a member of the ambulance crew finally arrived on the scene and took over, I'd never been so relieved to see anyone before in my life! After several failed attempts at resuscitating this man, the crew put him in the back of the ambulance, hit the blue lights and raced up to the North Staffs Royal Infirmary with him.

The crowd drifted away as I went to inspect the man's car and prepared to get it off the road. I soon saw clues as to why a relatively young man was having a heart attack: the car's ashtray was overflowing with cigarette ends and there was grey ash scattered all around the footwells.

I had just finished getting the car off the road and secured when I was radioed and asked to go to the hospital. Unfortunately, the man had died. They needed me to attend the hospital and take down the details.

When I got back to the station, I relayed the whole story to my colleagues. In a typical display of how we often used humour to diffuse tragic events, I got teased mercilessly for giving the deceased gentleman the "kiss of life"!

The police are notorious for teasing each other, and I noticed straight away that there was a never-ending stream of banter and name calling. Fortunately for me, the name that did stick was fairly inoffensive and emerged from a rather amusing story.

I was on foot patrol – known as "Lima Alpha Four One" – around Stoke town centre one day when I received a call on my radio. (This was before I did my driving course to enable me to drive the panda cars, something I was actually lucky enough to do before the end of my two-year probationary period – most people had to wait until their probationary period had ended.) I was informed that there had been several reports of what looked like a brightly coloured parrot flying around the area and perching on top of lampposts. I wasn't too far from the location, so I went to investigate. I was intrigued. I was also a bit puzzled. What was I going to do if I did see it? I couldn't imagine telling a parrot to come quietly!

I walked around the area for a while but couldn't see any parrot or distressed owner looking for an escaped parrot. I radioed in to say as much over the Lima Alpha airwaves. ("Lima Alpha" was the two-letter designated call sign for any patrol based at Stoke Police Station. Every police station has its very own two-letter call sign to indicate where the patrol and officers are from and their role. For example, CID, traffic patrols and dog handlers have their own specific call signs to allow control rooms and officers to identify them.) Over the airwaves came the announcement, "Thank you Lima Alpha, four one. We obviously sent the right patrol to that job, didn't we PC Tawney Howell?" He said it dropping the "H" so it sounded like "Tawny Owl" and that was it. Tawny was my nickname for the rest of my days at Stoke! In many ways, being given a nickname was a rite of passage, a feeling like you'd been accepted.

These were the days, incidentally, when every police station had its own control room rather than the one huge, central control room we have now. In those days, local controllers knew their "patch" and knew all the local characters in the community. The advantage of this was that it was harder for time wasters to pull the wool over our eyes. For example, if someone reported a potential drunk driver but wouldn't give their name, we knew it was likely a ruse to get someone they had a vendetta against into trouble. We would always investigate to a certain point to ensure we weren't missing any real crime that was being committed but if the moment came when we realised we were being led astray, we'd quickly let it go.

If every day could have involved me doing nothing riskier than looking for elusive parrots, I think my mother would have been much happier, because she was all too aware that, as a serving police officer, I might be injured in the line of duty in any number of ways. I count myself very lucky to have completed my career suffering nothing more serious than the odd scrape or bruise, and never needing to be admitted to hospital. The closest I ever came to it involved a story featuring another animal.

I was on duty one New Year's Eve when we received a call at around 4am that there was a house fire at a property on Whieldon Road. I had passed my driving course by then, so I jumped in a panda car with a special constable who I was partnered up with that night, hit the blue lights and raced to the scene. Special constables are people who volunteer their time to be police officers and support regular permanent officers. They receive some basic training and then accompany a permanent officer on patrol. They are drawn from the local community and generally have other "day jobs". Some special constables join to gain an insight into policing before deciding whether or not to join the police service full time. The vast majority of special constables simply want to serve their local community and I have always admired their commitment and dedication, and willingness to give their own time and to work voluntarily in this way.

When we arrived, we could see smoke billowing out of the front door and upstairs windows of the terraced property. A small crowd had congregated outside; some had escaped the burning property and others were neighbours watching the drama unfold. Some were wearing their dressing gowns, having been in bed and awoken by the commotion. Others were still in their party attire since it was the early hours of the New Year. Noticeably absent from this crowd was the fire service!

We immediately asked if everyone had made it out of the house and were relieved to hear that they had. However, someone piped up, "But the dog's still in there." I didn't budge as I knew that animals are notorious for getting themselves out of a burning property. However, before I could stop him, my colleague dashed through the smoke billowing out of the front door and disappeared into the house. Just as he vanished from sight, I heard the fire engine sirens coming up the road, and in the next moment, predictably, the dog came wandering out of the house.

He wasn't much to look at, this scrawny dog. He was what we colloquially referred to as a "Heinz" dog because he was a mongrel of debatable heritage and probably made up of around 57 varieties. (For younger readers, Heinz, the company that makes soups, sauces and baked beans, amongst other food items, was once very famously known as the food brand with "57 varieties"; that was their marketing slogan.) However, he was obviously very dear to his owner, who scooped him up and held tightly onto him. Now my concern grew for my colleague, who was nowhere to be seen. I took a few tentative steps into the house and started shouting through the dense smoke. I called numerous times but there was no answer. I grew extremely concerned and kept shouting as hard as I could. Where was he?

Finally, just as the first fireman arrived at the door, my

colleague emerged, coughing and spluttering, his face black with soot. We later found out that the fire had been caused by a deep fat fryer catching alight; that was why it was particularly thick and dirty, it was burning old chip fat. Apparently, the culprit had returned home, inebriated, and had decided he needed chips. He had started cooking them and then passed out. This was quite a common incident in the area, I learned.

My colleague was given oxygen and taken in an ambulance to the hospital. I followed in the panda car. When we arrived, the paramedics insisted that I took a blood test, too. This showed, to my horror, that I actually had higher blood gases than my colleague. I was told this was probably because I'd been shouting so much through the smoke and inhaling it that way. They wanted to admit me overnight but, as I was married to a nurse at the time, I persuaded them to let me go home where – I assured them – I would be very well looked after.

My colleague was released the next day without any major injuries but having learnt a valuable lesson the hard way: you never run into a burning house to rescue an animal!

The first major incident that I attended actually occurred in Lichfield, around 43 miles away from Stoke. It was in June 1990 and a solider had been shot and killed on the platform of Lichfield train station in a suspected IRA attack. This was at the height of IRA activity in the UK. Staffordshire was something of an epicentre for it at that time; a few months later, in September, they also attempted to kill the RAF's Air Chief Marshall, Sir Peter Terry, at his home in Milford, Staffordshire. Miraculously, he survived.

I was included in the huge team of officers who were

seconded from all parts of the Staffordshire police service and instructed to conduct interviews under the direction of the murder team. This was the largest investigation to date that had been conducted by Staffordshire Police and there were simply not enough officers stationed at the local police station in Lichfield to cope with the mass of evidence that had to be gathered from witnesses. No stone was to be left unturned, especially as there was so much media attention around it; the eyes of the country were watching as it was prime time news on the BBC and ITV. I'll never forget a most memorable moment during this period when I almost ran headlong into Kate Adie, the famous BBC war correspondent, as she was dashing down the staircase of Lichfield Police Station and I was running the opposite way. I definitely did that "double take" moment, thinking, "Wow, that really is Kate Adie, off the BBC News!"

The secondment lasted for about four weeks, during which I spent most of my time being driven around by an experienced detective in a grey Leyland Maestro van visiting witnesses and taking statements from them. My first experience of a major terrorist incident was a fascinating and exhilarating time. I thought of it many years later, when I was involved with another major terrorist incident in 2017.

I had a great start to my career at Stoke Police Station, gaining experience and confidence, and also gaining respect amongst my peers. I learnt a huge amount about myself in that time, too. I also put to bed some of the fears that my mother had passed on to me. She continued to worry and would have liked nothing more than to know I'd been given a desk job, but she also saw how happy I was, that I'd found my purpose and enjoyed my vocation, and I think that mattered to her more than peace of mind. The thought of me miserable, sitting behind a desk, would not have made her happy either. In total, I was at Stoke for nearly four years, and by the time I was due to move on, I was ready for a new environment and some more adventures. The best part of being in the police is the fact that you get to move on and try a different variety of roles and locations without having to leave your job. As I considered the many different jobs I could do, I felt particularly lucky in this.

I attended numerous courses during my time at Stoke, I had built up new skills and I was keen to start spreading my wings and seeing where my career would take me. I wanted to take on new challenges and keep learning. The courses I took included qualifying as a tutor constable (which means mentoring and being responsible for the development of probationary constables who have recently completed their initial training), learning how to drive a police car (which meant getting the keys to the station's "panda" cars) and how to operate the station's breathalyser machine.

The breathalyser course was the most interesting, and it's a shame that it no longer exists in the format that I experienced it. When I took it, it was an overnight course held at the then headquarters building in Stafford. The breathalyser machine itself was the size of a desk. It was designed to measure the amount of alcohol in the breath of a suspected drunk driver. This would be presented as legal evidence in court. Officers on breathalyser duty had the onerous task of handling a suspected drunk driver who had been arrested and booked into the station's custody suite. There were some real characters, but suspected drunk drivers came from all backgrounds, there wasn't a "type" as such. What was common was seeing most of them come to realise the full potential consequences of their actions, that they might be about to lose more than their driving licence, possibly also their livelihood, and even their marriage and home. Many shed tears as they began to imagine their life fading further and further away each time they exhaled the two requisite long breaths down a plastic tube, especially as they were often beginning to sober up by this time and starting to regret their actions. More often than not, these were people who had never even entered a police station before, let alone been in one in custody. I used to imagine them sitting there thinking, "It's not like this on *The Bill*," (the popular, long-running British police drama TV series).

So why was it an overnight course? For one simple reason: you were expected to get drunk! Or at least a little tipsy.

The first afternoon was spent learning the functionality of the actual machine, which was known as "The Box" and the various legal aspects of the using the device to get admissible evidence. The evening was spent in the bar, which was conveniently situated on the floor above the classroom where our training was being conducted. We were instructed to have a drink in the bar, wait 20 minutes, and then go and test ourselves or a colleague and monitor the results. This was going to make for an interesting evening, we all thought!

I had a total of three pints during the course of the evening. After each one, when it was my turn to put myself on The Box, I was fascinated to watch how the figures grew after each long blow down the plastic tube. After those three pints, I didn't need The Box to tell me that I would have been in no state to drive a car and yet, when I blew into the tube, The Box informed me that I would have been under the legal limit and thus officially allowed to drive. This was quite frightening and brought home to me how your capacity to process alcohol – and thus the reading given by The Box – was affected by so many more factors than simply how many drinks you'd had. They included your physical size and fitness, how often you drank, your gender, your sleep patterns, etc.

Throughout the course of my career, I changed the lives of many people from all walks of life, by breathalysing them and finding the evidence to ban them for driving for a time. They came in all shapes and sizes… some claiming they'd only had one pint when they were quite clearly wet through. Others seemed almost sober and yet they blew three or four – even five – times the legal limit! These were the type with major drinking problems, who could tolerate a huge amount of alcohol without seeming drunk. Those types were walking around all day almost permanently at the legal limit so one bottle of cider could tip them over the edge. So, when they said, "But I've only had a bottle of cider," they might have been telling the truth, but they were still over the limit.

I also thoroughly enjoyed the driving course. I am sure every probationer awaits their first police driving course with eager anticipation; it's a real watershed and turning point moment in any police officer's career. Being handed the keys to a panda car, knowing you will soon be skilfully weaving through traffic, speeding to an emergency to save life and limb with blue lights and sirens wailing, is that hallowed moment most of us longed for. The glory and the glamour!

The first driving course for all police officers is known as the "basic" driving course and authorises the successful trainee to drive those smaller station patrol cars: the Ford Escort fleet. Anyone wanting to move on to the traffic group and drive the high-performance cars has to apply for an "advanced" driving course, consisting of around five weeks of intense driving, pushing the driver and the car to their limits.

I was lucky to get the opportunity to do my driving course in March 1991, several months before my probationary period was due to end. I saw it as a positive sign, assuming that, if they were going to invest the time and money in me to get me through my driving course, I probably stood a good chance of remaining beyond those initial two probationary years, so I was particularly relieved when I was given the dates for my course.

Almost everyone who can drive assumes they drive well. But learning to drive as a police officer takes your driving skills to a whole new level. One of the things I learned from this experience is that, no matter how skilled you think you already are at something, there is always more to learn. I was certain I could drive well and would sail through the course, but there were so many new experiences, so much I had to learn. I'd passed my regular driving test about three years before and I was a fairly confident driver, but this course included a lot more of the theory as well as the physical technique. We were taught to make forward observations and how to think our way around what might happen, in order to respond to our predictions as well as moment-by-moment situations in real time. I doubt the general public gives much thought to the officers behind the wheels of the police cars dashing around town centres, but they have all been trained to very high standards in order to give them the best chance of reducing risk.

Much like my probationary foundation course, the structure of the driving course had only recently been changed when I came to take it, so I was a guinea pig once again. The advanced driving course used to be run as a residential course that would take two weeks but that had been abandoned in favour of running the course as a series of lessons, just as you would have when preparing for a regular driving test. The instructor would pick me up during an "early" or "noon" shift and take me for a one-hour lesson. There were pros and cons to this. On the one hand, if my lesson was at the end of a run of "earlies" (the 6am—2pm shift), I wasn't always at my best. Four early shifts in a row and the last thing I felt like doing was concentrating on new driving skills. But on the other hand, this gave me "realtime" experience. If I could drive at speed when I was dog tired after four early shifts in a row, hopefully I'd be able to drive under pressure any time.

Another challenge was manoeuvring the traditional "panda cars", which were unlike the modern vehicles the police drive today. In those days we drove around in a very basic Ford Escort with a small 1.3 litre petrol engine, known as a "panda car". A few traffic cones and possibly a "Police Stop" or "Accident" sign would be thrown into the boot along with a very basic first aid kit. This was the era when the much more powerful Ford Fiesta XR2 and the Ford Cosworth were the cars of choice for the local joy riders and "ram raiders" (groups of car thieves who would steal a car, ram it into the front of a shop, smashing the windows and then raid the goods – usually alcohol and cigarettes but also clothing and other goods). Any time we had to pursue a stolen one of those high-performance vehicles, the little engine of the Ford Escort would be driven to its limit to keep them in sight.

I was also introduced, at this time, to the bible of police driving, Roadcraft. Printed in a similar format to the Highway Code, this document gives instruction on how to drive "to the system" and had to be learnt inside out. "The System" is a set of procedures written specifically for police drivers, a set of instructions that you have to learn, like learning "mirror, signal, manoeuvre" when you first learn to drive… but a little more intense! To pass the police driving test we were told we had to know the book inside out and back-to-front, and then drive exactly as the book dictated. I memorised "the system" so well, there are parts that I can still remember today, after nearly 30 years; I have no doubt the majority of police officers, serving and retired, can do the same.

One of the most valuable skills I learnt during this course was the ability to control a car that is skidding. For this we practised on the police driving school's "skid pan", which was situated just outside Stafford at a village called Hixon. A skid pan is a circular area of tarmac about the size of two tennis courts. The area of tarmac is like an inverted dome, with a gentle gradient sloping down to the centre where there is a drain. The ground is covered with oil and water and we were made to drive old unmarked patrol cars, with no tread on their tyres, across it, sometimes having to swerve around cones that were strategically placed in our way. Learning to control a skidding car is one of those skills that can benefit any driver; it could mean the difference between life and death in some situations. I was always aware that this particular course was not only going to benefit my police career, but it might be of critical use any day, any time, and could well give me the skills to protect my own family if a dangerous situation ever arose on the roads.

As with any course, so much of its value is in the delivery, the quality of the teaching and the rapport you have with the instructor. I was very lucky in that I had a great instructor with whom I got on very well. I thoroughly enjoyed the challenges of learning my advanced driving skills, and I believe they have benefitted me in my career and everyday life.

I will never forget the moment when I was told I'd passed my driving course. In the same way as regular driving tests are organised – with the driving instructor passing responsibility over to an elected examiner, with the police driving test, the instructor gives way to a police sergeant from the police driving school; this is a little added pressure in an already tense situation. My examiner had a check sheet attached to a wooden clip board and made notes as we toured the streets of Stafford in a plain white Ford Escort for the best part of an hour. It was a huge relief when he eventually informed me that I had passed. I remember feeling particularly glad that I hadn't let my instructor down and that I wouldn't be ridiculed for having not passed. I was also especially pleased to think that I would be able to assist my colleagues in answering emergency calls. More than anything, it confirmed that I was "in", that I was going to be a "real" police officer.

CHAPTER FOUR:

PC HOWELL

Shortly after my probationary period ended and I was a fully-fledged "officer of the law" I was offered the chance to train as a tutor constable myself. To be given the opportunity at such an early stage of my career was a real honour and I was overjoyed at the opportunity to build on the great experience I'd had with the tutor constable who'd been such a valuable support to me. I was well aware that being asked to nurture a new officer through some of the most challenging moments of their training and influential times of their career was a big responsibility, but it gave me an opportunity to continue my own learning. And it was at this point that I realised how perfectly policing suited me, because it's a career where you can learn something new almost every day. It's not a job you can easily get bored in!

During my time as a tutor constable, I only ever had one probationary constable, but the experience provided me with further invaluable experiences and insights, in particular into the issue of racism. The officer I tutored was an Indian woman and, while I never saw any racism aimed at her from colleagues, I was shocked by some of the attitudes towards her I witnessed coming from the general public. The first of these happened when we had to take a statement from the owner of a petrol station who'd been the victim of a "drive off" (when a motorist fills up with petrol and drives off without paying). The exercise proved extremely difficult. The man, who was also from an Asian background, simply would not conduct the conversation with my colleague. He directed everything towards me, and when we left the garage, she explained that this was because she was an Indian female and he was a Pakistani male, and he could not accept her having a position of authority over him.

My young protégé further opened my eyes when she explained how hard it had been for her to join the police. Her family were totally against it and felt she'd brought shame on them; they did not feel it was an appropriate career for an Indian woman. But she was resolute in her ambition to become a police officer and I admired her courage. I was alarmed to learn, several years later, that she had been kidnapped by her family and taken to India. However, I wasn't surprised to further learn that this unstoppable brave woman managed to break free, get herself back to England and returned to working with the Staffordshire police. What a tenacious spirit!

When the time came for me to seek promotion, I had to think deeply about what I wanted to do. The natural next step was to go into CID (Criminal Investigation Department), which meant leaving "the streets" and putting my days in uniform behind me. But I liked being directly involved with the public and where the "action" happened. Using initiative and ingenuity to prevent crime before it happened gave me the greatest job satisfaction. Helping the people of Staffordshire in their hours of need was the primary reason I joined the police force. On a personal level, I had also particularly enjoyed my driving course so when the opportunity arose to join "the Traffic" I jumped at the chance. I had actually passed my "basic" driving course before attending the tutor course as this was a requirement for the tutor course: you had to be able to drive in order to provide the new recruit the experience of answering calls in a vehicle as well as on foot. Once a probationary constable had been authorised to patrol alone, their solo patrols would be on foot so that they could gain more experience by walking around Stoke town centre and the surrounding back streets.

Opting to join the traffic police meant another driving course, the "advanced" driving course, which was probably one of the most demanding and challenging courses I took in my career. You didn't just have your own driving to experience but the driving of two other students. At the Weston Road training centre situated on the outskirts of Stafford, we were placed in groups of three students with an instructor and when one student was driving, the other two became passengers. But this was not exactly like being chauffeured around in a luxury limousine! While each student drove, the others had to stay exceptionally alert and attentive to what was going on. We had to stick to speed restrictions in 30, 40 or 50 mph areas but once we were on a road where the national speed limit (60mph on single carriageway country roads, and 70mph on motorways) was in force, we were expected to drive as quickly, but as safely, as possible. We were instructed to go as fast as we could, and heart rates would rise with the speedometer.

Our instructor on this course was a real character and mostly cheerful, except for that one time.

I was behind the wheel and we were driving up a fairly steep ascent on a country road in the Cotswolds. There were two lines going in our direction of travel and one lane coming towards us in the other direction. I knew the two lanes were merging ahead and I was stuck behind quite a slow lorry. I thought I saw the opportunity to overtake but as I did, I realised I was running out of lane and there was a car coming towards us. I tried to slow down but the lorry had slowed to let me overtake him so I found myself trapped in a dance where no one knew which move to make next, a bit like when you meet someone on a path coming towards you and you both step out of the way but end up still facing each other and you do that little dance, shuffling back and forth. But this was slightly different in that we were travelling in fast moving vehicles.

I hit the accelerator and somehow managed to squeeze through the gap between the lorry and the oncoming vehicle but not without using the last bit of space on the road which was covered in the white chevrons telling you to merge.

The instructor told me to pull over as soon as I could. I pulled up in the next lay-by and he turned to me – not so jovial anymore – and spoke words that became etched on my brain forever. Simply, "You put us in danger. Don't do that again."

I never did!

★

I had to pinch myself to believe that I was really being paid to hurtle around the roads of Staffordshire and beyond in a white unmarked advanced car, either a Jaguar or Vauxhall Senator, learning skills I'd never even imagined, such as driving on an oiled skidpan. Again, these skills become ingrained in you for life, which only helps keep you and others on the road safer when you're driving.

Then there was the day we went to the seaside. The objective was to enable us to experience a long, fast drive at night, the conditions in which we were most likely to be having to do the majority of our high-speed driving. We drove to Barmouth in North Wales just in time to get fish and chips before the place closed. Then we drove home. I wasn't behind the wheel on this occasion, it was one of the other students, who was adept at driving exceptionally fast. His ability to handle the three-litre Senator was eye-watering and he rounded corners on the windy and cold grey Welsh roads expertly. I was in awe of his skills as I sat behind him in the car; the lampposts along the M54 from Telford to Stafford on our return journey literally seemed to whistle past my window as we reached 145mph. When we got back to base at Weston Road, our instructor informed us that this was the fastest he'd ever been driven by a student driver and remarked that we had, on occasions, "lived on the very edge of tyre technology!"

Once I'd passed my advanced driving course, I didn't return to Stoke, as I'd expected, but remained at Weston Road as part of the Central Traffic Group. At that time (1994), there were three traffic bases across Staffordshire responsible for policing the roads – Central (Stafford), Southern (Lichfield) and Northern (Hanley, Stoke). Central was the only base patrolling the motorways and covered the M6 and M54 within Staffordshire's county borders. This promised to be a new policing challenge for me, quite a change from buzzing around Stoke in a yellow and white Ford Escort dealing with domestic violence, bicycle thefts and Doulton breaks, but change was what I thrived on and a large part of the reason I'd joined the police.

A few months after transferring to the Central Traffic Group, I found myself back on the Telford to Stafford stretch of the M54 but this time a passenger in a fully marked police Vauxhall Senator, whilst my colleague drove. We were in pursuit (we were trained not to say "chasing") of a speeding motorcyclist. And I will never forget the moment I radioed our control room with the following message: "Tango Bravo three, three, we are pursuing a motorcycle M54 westbound towards Telford. Speed is one, five, zero miles per hour." The controller went quiet for a moment and then asked me to repeat, which I promptly did. To be honest, I needed convincing myself!

Even at that speed, we lost the motorcycle. I couldn't believe it as I saw its red rear light disappear from view as it headed into the unlit section of the motorway. We would have had to call for backup, even a helicopter, had we not noticed the offending vehicle lying on its side at the top of the Junction 3 slip road. The rider had hit some wet tarmac and slid off. Dishevelled and humiliated but otherwise unhurt, we arrested him on suspicion of having stolen the motorcycle and took him to Cannock Police Station.

We later found out that the motorcyclist was in the Royal Air Force riding back to his RAF station at Cosford. He received a hefty fine and driving ban, along with the somewhat dishonourable accolade of recording the fastest ever speed on the M54 at that time.

It wasn't all high-speed pursuits and adrenaline-producing events, there were also moments of humour, the downright bizarre and the mundane: all came in equal measures. One night shift involved redirecting a very elderly lady and her husband off the motorway after they inadvertently found themselves on the M6, having become disorientated in roadworks on the adjoining A5. She had never driven on the motorway and was terrified. She just stopped on the hard shoulder. And after a while we were alerted. The M6 is a daunting road at the best of times. After calming the distraught lady down, we told her to follow our police car. All went smoothly, albeit at a sedate speed. I kept her car in my sights in the patrol car's rear window to ensure that we didn't lose her. We eventually left the motorway and pulled over onto the hard shoulder to wave them on their journey. However, as we pulled onto the hard shoulder and illuminated our blue lights, she pulled over, too, rather than carry on.

What was wrong now?

I went to investigate again. As I approached, she wound down the front passenger window. The lady beamed up at me and I remember her words clearly.

"Thank you, so much young man, for all your help," she said. "Would you like a boiled sweet?" I gladly took two boiled sweets. One for me and one for my colleague. It wasn't every day we got appreciation like that.

Another bizarre experience was when we were asked to assist a botanist who had been employed to conduct a survey of the plants and trees adorning the embankments of the motorway in readiness for future expansion plans.

The botanist had found what he believed to be cannabis being grown on the embankment.

When we went to investigate, we found the plants exactly where and as the botanist had described. We put out word for any patrol passing this particular area of the motorway to pay "passing attention" and if any vehicles were stopped on the hard shoulder to stop and check them out. We also passed on this information to the local police station at Cannock which bordered the motorway, in case it resonated with anything happening in their area. We pulled the plants out of the ground, placed them in a black bin liner and put them into the boot of our patrol car for destruction on our return to base. To my knowledge, the mystery of the "phantom embankment cannabis grower" remains unsolved.

Another incident occurred when I was patrolling the northern section of the M6 motorway, from Stafford all the way to the county boundary with Cheshire at junction 16. Once again it was a Sunday night shift and I received a radio message to be on the alert for two high-powered cars that seemed to be racing one another north on the M6 motorway. The motorway cameras in the West Midlands had spotted them travelling at high speed but as they had no patrols to send, they simply alerted Staffordshire Police.

My colleague and I decided to wait and keep observations at Keele services, just north of junction 15, on the outskirts of Stoke-on-Trent, to see if they would come flying past. And flying past they came! One very nice BMW and one impressive looking Mercedes. We immediately alerted the control room that we had spotted the cars and that they were travelling, in tandem, at speeds of well in excess of 100mph. It was now about 2am. Suspecting the cars were stolen there was also a high chance that neither vehicle would stop, when requested to do so.

Catching up with the cars, we immediately noticed that both cars were displaying foreign number plates. German, in fact. They were both left-hand drive vehicles. Carefully positioning our patrol vehicle in between the BMW and the Mercedes, I illuminated the patrol car's blue lights to stop them. To our relief and amazement, both cars slowed and were guided to a stop on the hard shoulder. My colleague and I split up and I went to speak to the Mercedes driver whilst my colleague went to the BMW.

Having conducted a speed check on both vehicles we had calculated their speed in excess of 125mph but, as they were European, we would be unable to issue them with the usual fixed penalty notice. We had no other option other than to arrest them and take them to a nearby police station, which in this case would be Longton Police Station in Stoke-on-Trent. Further investigation found that both cars were indeed stolen.

During the subsequent interviews with the drivers, we gleaned that they were both mechanics from Italy and had driven the cars from Spain to Germany and then into to the UK, arriving on a ferry having crossed the English Channel. They had been heading towards Liverpool when we upset their plans. The belief was that the two cars were being driven to Liverpool to then be transported to Africa in a shipping container. Apparently, this was a normal route for stolen cars from the Continent that had been "stolen to order".

During the magistrates' court hearing, things took yet another twist and a very sleek and smartly presented solicitor appeared. Bail was offered if a certain amount of money was paid as a surety of the men's reappearance in the future, once further investigations into the car's history had been conducted. The solicitor pulled out of his smartly cut and expensive jacket what I can only describe as a "wedge" of bank notes and, without blinking an eye, paid the men's sureties and speeding fines. And that was the end of that.

CHAPTER FIVE:

TRAFFIC ON THE GROUND

I am sure all police officers who have worked in Traffic will agree that you never forget the first time you attend a fatal accident. My first time was in the early hours of the morning towards the end of a night shift and, but for a stroke of luck, could have also been the last time I attended any accident or incident!

We had heard reports that there was debris on the northbound carriageway of the M6 motorway, just before it splits off from the M6 at Junction 10A. We were the second patrol vehicle to arrive on the scene, where we discovered that the "debris" was the scattered remains of a Citroën Saxo.

I positioned my car perpendicular to the direction of traffic, across both of the inside lanes and facing the central barrier, to help cordon off the crew working at the scene and busied myself with ensuring there was as much protection for them as possible as more and more people arrived; the fire service, both of our shift sergeants, an ambulance crew and a patrol from West Midlands, as we were just a few hundred yards over the border from their jurisdiction.

The most poignant thing I learnt at this moment, and would continue to observe throughout my career, was that there are those people who have no problem looking at and dealing with severely or fatally wounded bodies and those, like me, who prefer not to. I think it's important, in the police service, to have both. You need the person who can go and pick up the body parts as well as the person who can sit with the grieving survivors and offer them comfort. Maybe this is similar to the slight dissociation a surgeon needs in order to perform open-heart surgery and the compassionate bedside manner a nurse needs in order to offer soothing words to someone in pain.

With everyone performing their tasks, I took on the task of radioing in the details of the car so that our control room could find out the owner of the vehicle, which might lead us to be able to identify the driver. A perfectly safe task, you might assume. Well, moments after I'd finished the call and had walked away from my vehicle and back to the accident scene, I heard an enormous bang, which I immediately identified as the sound of metal on metal, immediately followed by the sound of shattering glass. I spun around to see that my car had been shunted around 180 degrees so it was now facing the hard shoulder, and the front driver's side was all smashed up. Had I not walked away from the vehicle when I did, had I stayed in it for, literally, thirty seconds longer, I would have been in it at the time of impact and probably would have been a "write-off" like my car!

The driver of a small white van had somehow failed to see the overhead warning signs, the blue flashing lights of a gathering of emergency vehicles or the barrier of plastic cones cordoning off two lanes that he had smashed through before making impact with my car. He walked out of his van dazed but unscathed, although I later discovered he'd been given a five-year ban for dangerous driving. He was lucky he hadn't been responsible for killing a police officer on duty, too.

I was lucky that day, too, of course, unlike the driver of the Citroën Saxo who had been killed outright. A lengthy investigation concluded that he'd fallen asleep at the wheel but as there were no witnesses or CCTV footage, little else could be ascertained as to the exact nature of events that had led to him hitting the barrier of the hard shoulder at a speed and angle that had launched his vehicle into the air, flipping it and slicing its roof off, which had killed the driver instantly. The investigation uncovered that the driver was a soldier who'd been on an exercise which had involved him driving an armoured vehicle on Salisbury Plain for a lengthy amount of time. It seemed he had probably not had his allotted rest time before trying to drive home to his family who lived in the north west. On the day my life was spared by a twist of fate, his had been ended. Had I not stepped out of my car moments before it had been hit, I would have probably perished that day. Had he slept a few more hours or hit the barrier at a different angle, he might have survived. This profound experience has stayed with me, giving me perspective on how precious and fleeting life truly is.

A police officer's shift is never over until it's over, and if we thought we'd had enough drama for one night, we were wrong. There was one more incident that required our attention before we got back to base.

It was nearly 5.30 am as we the pulled off the M6 motorway at junction 14. On the hard shoulder of the relatively short slip road, we saw a red Ford Sierra estate car parked up with its boot wide open and three people on the ground, presumably trying to change a flat tyre. The car was in a dangerous position as the slip road wasn't well lit, so we pulled up behind it and switched on our roof lights to illuminate the scene. Once we were out of our patrol car, however, I immediately felt that instinct – call it a police officer's "sixth sense" – that all was not above board.

I sensed, as we approached the vehicle, that our presence was particularly irksome to the three men we could now clearly see who were in the process of changing a tyre. They did not seem keen to engage in conversation and I soon saw a possible reason why.

In the back of the car we could see several large black holdalls, I estimated six in total. I casually asked what they contained and after a suspiciously lengthy pause, one of the men answered that they contained cigarettes. I asked him to open the bags and, sure enough, they contained countless cartons of cigarettes. Far more than one person could smoke in a year so it was obvious they were intended for resale, and we finally got them to confess that they'd driven across to France where they'd bought the tax-free cigarettes and were on their way back to Lancashire to sell on their contraband.

This was not a case for us but for Customs and Excise. Once the tyre had been changed, we instructed them to follow us to the closest police station, where we contacted HM Customs and waited there for the officers to arrive to deal with the would-be smugglers. We later found out that the men had not been arrested by the Customs officers, but they had been bailed to appear at court in order to answer to magistrates. The cigarettes were confiscated and destroyed.

End of story.

But not quite.

Two nights later, at the start of my shift, we were travelling north to patrol the northern section of the M6 up to the Cheshire border. We joined the motorway at junction 14 and as we filtered into the traffic from the slip road, I did a double take. I could not believe it; we were driving behind the same Ford Sierra estate! Even before we'd checked the number plate, I remembered it from our last encounter.

We stayed behind the car at a reasonable distance until Keele Services, where we pulled it over at the police post there. The three occupants looked highly disgruntled when they realised that they were being stopped, and astonished as it dawned on them why my face looked familiar! And, lo and behold, we discovered the boot filled with holdalls again. And, yes, inside the holdalls were several hundred cartons of cigarettes. I had to pinch myself, I thought I was having a déjà vu. I'm sure the three men felt the same. Having driven straight back to France in an attempt to recover their losses after their last haul was confiscated, what were the chances that they would find themselves pulled over by the very same patrol they'd been foiled by the first time? Probably slimmer than winning the lottery. I almost felt sorry for them.

For the first and, so far only, time in my life, I was offered a bribe. One of the gang members took me to one side, took out a wad of rolled-up bank notes and quietly asked if we could come to "some arrangement". My answer, of course, was an emphatic "no!" The wad of money was shortly to be confiscated, along with another haul of contraband cigarettes, by HM Customs and Excise officers.

These were some of the more dramatic and interesting moments, but I soon realised that policing the motorway was not for me. For the most part working in Traffic, especially on the motorway, was very sterile. It wasn't what I got into policing for. There were some fantastic people working on the team but patrolling the same piece of road, day in, day out, and spending half my time with my neck twisted around, looking over my right shoulder for speeding vehicles, was not my idea of fun. There was so little interaction with people. When we stopped people for speeding, we gave them a ticket and they went on their way. It had ruined their day, so it was a thankless task. And there was no nuance, I couldn't put my stamp on anything by personalising how I dealt with a problem. I missed the ins and outs, the colourfulness, of helping people deal with difficulties they'd run into in the course of their everyday lives. I knew from very early on that this wouldn't be the area I'd want to stay in for too long. I needed a change of scene.

As is so often the case in life, once you "put it out there" – as in, start thinking about changing direction – an opportunity seems to present itself out of nowhere.

I was on a regular night shift and at our 10pm briefing, our sergeant made a request for someone to help out at Traffic Support South (that covered the southern parts of Staffordshire) at the base at Lichfield. They were short staffed and needed some help for a couple of nights. I jumped at the opportunity. It meant a little further to commute to work, but I couldn't pass up the chance to do something new. Traffic Support South covered three large geographical areas comprising Cannock, Lichfield and Tamworth, Burton and Uttoxeter, as well as parts of the A5 and the A38. A larger area covered by fewer officers. I relished the new challenges that this might bring.

The following night, I reported to Lichfield Police Station. The traffic group was tucked away at the far end of the station, and since there were fewer officers there was less supervision, which meant – I soon discovered – that they had a much closer and more symbiotic relationship with all the local police stations in the areas they covered than we had with ours. The whole approach was different. Everyone helped each other, which meant that, even though we were technically only responsible for traffic policing, we did get involved with other incidents. In particular, we were encouraged to follow up on any leads we got; we were given a lot of autonomy. For example, if we suspected that a disqualified driver was still driving, despite having been banned for a time by the courts, we could conduct surveillance in unmarked cars and arrest them. We could also pass that information about the driver and vehicle on to local stations, which would help them build their intelligence on criminals in the area.

I also gained a perspective on how my original group – the Central Traffic Group – was viewed from another perspective. I discovered that, being well staffed and equipped with better vehicles, we were viewed as the "spoilt ones". There was also a perception that "motorway officers" thought they were a cut above officers who worked "in the sticks", so there was that stigma, too.

On my first shift, I was crewed up with a colleague who'd been at Traffic Support South for some time and we were assigned to the Cannock division. We had an eventful night involving the prolonged pursuit of a vehicle that took us up and down the A5 and M54 several times. A convoy of vehicles from neighbouring forces of Staffordshire, West Midlands and West Mercia became involved in the operation. We decided to try using a stinger unit. This involves getting in front of the vehicle in question and finding a safe place to lay down a trellis type instrument containing hundreds of tiny hollow nails positioned across its framework. When the suspect vehicle drives over it, the tyres are punctured, bringing the vehicle to a fairly abrupt stop.

We managed to get in front of the vehicle by using a parallel road and found a suitable place that would soon be in its path where we could throw the stinger into the road. My colleague carried the stinger up a grass verge and lay in wait. However, as the vehicle approached, the driver obviously saw him and attempted to drive up the verge and swerve around him. He jumped out of the way and attempted to throw the stinger under the car. He managed to get it under the rear nearside tyre: a partial success.

As the pursuit continued, the damaged car and the pursuing pack of police vehicles was reminiscent of a nature documentary where a buffalo has been partially wounded but is still trying to outrun a pack of hungry, bloodthirsty hyenas chasing it; the hyenas following with the confidence that the beast will soon tire and slow down, which is when they intend to pounce and devour it. Our attempt to "spear" the tyres had not been entirely successful, but we had done just enough to wound the fleeing beast and eventually the pack got their prey.

We soon learned that the driver was in custody and felt relieved that there had been a safe resolution to what was potentially a dangerous and life-threatening situation. Later we discovered that the woman was having a psychotic episode due to a mental illness. This is the kind of detail that the public are so often unaware of. Police chases in TV shows and films usually involve bank robbers, or teenagers taking a high-powered sports car for a spin. Reality is often very different and many "crimes" are committed by people who are seriously unwell and need professional help.

After two night-shifts at Traffic Support South, I knew this was where I wanted to be and I asked to be transferred to Lichfield. After a short period, my request was granted and I started some of my most enjoyable years of policing. I immediately enjoyed the variety of the work, the involvement with so many different people, and being more involved with preventing crime in conjunction with officers at different stations. It was far more interesting than simply patrolling the motorways. Although my motorway patrolling days were not quite over: I had not seen the last of the M6.

I got lucky from day one as I joined what was arguably the best shift, known as "Shift 3". The culture of a shift team is, for the most part, created by the sergeant in charge of it and, quite simply, we had a great sergeant. There was plenty of literature that came down to us from on high... colourful posters and vision statements about what they wanted the "culture of policing" to look like, but culture cannot be artificially imposed by faceless bureaucrats, it must be created from within an organisation, with everyone taking part in shaping it. It is something that can be informed by directives, but it must grow organically. I can't say I fully understood this dynamic myself at that exact moment; it is something I came to understand over time. I did, however, understand some basic principles of human behaviour. My mother taught me a very simple one: treat people as you would like to be treated yourself. This served me well for the most part. The more complex principles about human behaviour and the culture of organisations I would come to experience later in my career.

Our sergeant on "Shift 3" at Litchfield, Sgt Paul Harris, also consolidated some practices in me. He had a strong ethical code and was a stickler for discipline, but he was also respectful to individuals and empathetic. He treated us humanely and had human qualities himself. His mood was known to fluctuate but we always had prior warning by how many sugars he requested in his tea. Someone – generally the most recent person to join the shift – would offer everyone a tea or coffee at the start of a shift. If the sergeant asked for two sugars in his drink, we knew his mood was okay, but it he asked for three or more, we knew it was going to be a bit of a bumpy shift, and it would not be the day for trying to get a less-than-perfect report past him or ask for annual leave.

Our sergeant was a stickler for rules because he believed we all had a responsibility to support each other, as a team. For example, if anyone forgot to sign out a patrol vehicle's "kit" (a large plastic box containing items you might require during your shift, including a tyre gauge, a breathalyser and a tape measure) they were made to feel that they had let the whole team down. But the opposite always applied, with those who did a job well being praised for having positioned the whole team in a good light. Even if a conventional line hadn't quite been followed, if we'd achieved our aims and no one got hurt, he stood by us. He set the basic parameters, but we knew we could push them if we were confident of a positive outcome. I remember one such occasion well.

We had just started our shift at 10pm when we got the call over the radio that a local police patrol was in pursuit of a stolen red Vauxhall Cavalier whose occupants had just burgled a clothes shop in Burton. The vehicle was heading south along the A38 and towards Lichfield. We abandoned our steaming cups of tea and coffee and jumped into action. Within minutes, five cars were speeding towards the A38 with sirens blaring and blue lights flashing. We split up so as to cover all possible routes of the Cavalier once it hit Lichfield where the A38 diverged into different routes around the town. My colleague (who was driving) and I decided to head to where the A38 crosses the A5 at Hints Island, south of Lichfield, to wait. Our sergeant, who was positioned further north than ourselves, along with another patrol car, waited where the A38 splits at the A5148 at Swinfen, so they saw the vehicle first and alerted everyone as they set off in pursuit of it.

When we heard over the radio that the stolen vehicle was heading south towards us, we decided to drive around the large roundabout, intending to join the convoy at the back of the pursuing police cars. But things didn't quite go to plan.

Just as we set off around the roundabout, we encountered the stolen red Cavalier coming straight towards us! We were on course for a head-on collision. Luckily my colleague's instincts kicked in and he managed to swerve. But not before I'd let out an almighty scream (one of the very few times I did in the course of my career) and almost leapt out of my seat to join him in his! Some form of divine intervention – and good driving skills by my colleague – got us out of the way, and we carried on around the roundabout, managing to join it at the junction it was exiting at, getting alongside it as we sped down the westbound lane of the A5.

Moments later, the front nearside of our patrol car came into contact with the rear offside of the Cavalier, which lurched violently to its nearside. In a sequence that would have been put into slow motion in an action film's police chase climax, the Cavalier clipped the high concrete kerb, sending it across our path at an acute and unnatural angle over to the opposite kerb, where it bounced off, rolled over twice, narrowly missed a large tree stump, crashed through a hedge and landed on its roof in a field.

The two occupants scrambled out of the car so dizzy and disorientated that one of them ran straight towards us. The other escaped into the surrounding woodland but was caught within hours, looking desperately dishevelled.

Our patrol car also looked very sorry for itself by the time we got it back to the station. There was some collateral damage and it hadn't been a conventional pursuit, but we had two people in custody, had recovered stolen goods (the clothes were fine, the Cavalier was a write-off) and no one had been seriously hurt. Other sergeants might have criticised us, but our sergeant backed us every step of the way. That was the kind of leader he was. He had our backs.

Our antics also had a positive knock-on effect. We heard on the grapevine that criminal gangs from Birmingham (which is where the Cavalier thieves were from) worked out which nights the "Shift 3" from Traffic Support South were working by following our shift patterns for a few weeks, and wouldn't risk venturing out on those nights, deciding they were no match for such a maverick, "ruthless" team. We had a real "Band of Brothers" camaraderie. Coming into work had a good vibe about it. Many of us arrived early to prepare and also catch up with each other over a joke or anecdote. We were sent to our patrol areas comfortable in the knowledge that, any time we needed help and assistance, we would be there for each other. That support extended to our private lives when issues we were facing invariably became entangled with work.

If I thought my motorway patrolling days were over by being transferred to Traffic Support South, I was much mistaken. I was to find myself on the M6 again, on one particularly infamous and unforgettable day, not long after joining the group. The day was Friday 4th April 1997, and the IRA had planted a bomb under an electricity pylon near Junction 9 on the southbound carriageway. With fears about the possibility of the high-voltage cables falling across the motorway running high, traffic was at a complete standstill. My former colleagues at Central Traffic needed assistance and as I was working on the Cannock patrol area, I was tasked with driving to where the border between Staffordshire and West Midlands crossed the M6 between junction 10 and 10A. I was instructed to close the border by putting my car across the three lanes of the southbound carriageway so that no more cars could travel any further south.

I followed instructions, expecting the usual irate tirades of drivers frustrated with being preventing from going about their business. However, something was completely different that day. There seemed to be almost a "Dunkirk spirit", a real acceptance that this incident was serious, beyond our control and the police were only doing their best to keep people safe. People helped each other deal with the wait, which was particularly hard to be patient with when a decision was taken to turn traffic around and get them off the motorway at Junction 11. This had to be done systematically and carefully. Cars that were closest to me were suddenly at the back of the queue and were going to have a long time to wait.

Of course, the roads feeding off the motorway soon became pretty solid, too, and it took all day to get the vehicles off that stretch of the M6. At one point, the Superintendent came to offer his support to keep up the spirits of the "troops". I remember he turned up with a quip about wishing he hadn't put his "dancing shoes" on that morning because he'd ended up walking for miles along the M6 tarmac. And later, the West Midlands traffic crew turned up to lend a hand. I remember they had thick black marks around their nostrils. They looked like the chimney sweeps from Mary Poppins and I naively asked if they'd been attending a fire. They told me it was simply soot from the exhaust fumes they'd been enveloped in as they'd walked amongst the cars, speaking with motorists further south on the motorway. If that was the effect of being around stationary traffic after only a few hours, what would the effect of years and years of working on the motorway be? I felt more relieved than ever that I'd left the motorway group.

The excitement of working as a police officer, for me, was always about the element of surprise. You really never knew, from one moment to the next, where the work might take you.

I remember a call I took one morning about an armed robbery. It had happened at the post office in Shenstone, an affluent village about 5 miles south of Lichfield, on the way to Sutton Coldfield. An armed man had robbed the post office. After pointing a gun at terrified staff, he'd forced them to hand over cash and had then made off on a bicycle.

By the time I got the call, several police cars had been dispatched to go in search of the suspect. I was being drafted in to cover more ground. Once I heard where they were heading, I decided to go in a different direction, to the far side of the village, assuming the man couldn't have got that far on a bicycle and also might have transferred to travelling on foot. This was one of those occasions I decided to play the tactic of being the "10th man". Everyone had assumed he'd gone in a certain direction, so I saw it as my duty to cover an entirely different one.

I parked up in a country lane and waited. Before long, I saw a young man carrying a rucksack sauntering towards me on the offside verge. I approached him and asked him where he was going. He seemed extremely nervous. He gave me a plausible explanation, but something didn't feel right. My sixth sense was telling me to question him further.

I invited him to come and sit with me in my patrol car and he reluctantly agreed. I then radioed for a local patrol to join me; I wanted a second opinion. He agreed that the man did match the sketchy description given by the traumatised post office staff and we decided to arrest him on suspicion of the robbery.

Once he was in custody, it was CID's job to establish if he was actually the bicycle robber. It was obvious he was but after several interviews he had to be released and bailed; there was simply insufficient evidence to charge him. However, the CID made a smart move; they called in the surveillance team, who followed the man back to Shenstone. He headed straight to the local churchyard, where he uncovered a stash of bank notes from behind a gravestone. Gotcha! He was re-arrested.

I was praised and actually received an official "commendation" for my role in the arrest. It was my initiative that had landed me in the location where the man was walking. If I hadn't gone there, he may well have evaded capture. It was a good lesson in how thinking outside of the box can often bring positive results. It was a strategy I used at other moments throughout my police career. I always asked myself whether I wanted to follow the crowd or go my own way. When I got the opportunity to "act up" as sergeant for my shift, I was determined to think more creatively whenever I could.

I had been at Traffic Support South for a few years when our popular shift sergeant was promoted to inspector. I had recently passed my sergeant's exams and they asked me to fill the role until a permanent sergeant could be recruited.

When I started my police career, the promotion process used to be based solely on a traditional "school exam" style written essay. By the time I came to take my sergeant's exams, it had become a two-stage process. Stage one was a multiple-choice test, which we had to pass first before going onto a practical, scenario-based exam. This involved spending about five minutes reading the given details of a scenario – all the circumstances surrounding an event, be it dealing with a member of the public wanting to complain about the police or advising a police constable about a disciplinary procedure – and then having 10 minutes in which to deal with the situation, while the examiners assessed us. This was all done using role play, which I found very stressful and unrealistic. But I passed, which qualified me to "act up" as sergeant for my shift.

I was honoured to be given the opportunity although I was introduced, for the first time in my life, to the experience of "imposter syndrome", a state of mind where you suffer from a lack of confidence, convincing yourself that someone has given you a job "by mistake" and they will soon discover you are an imposter. I would study this psychological condition much later in life.

At the time, I was confronted with all the fears about whether I could manage a team of officers with all their personal quirks, egos, ambitions, opinions and experience. I knew it would be a challenge but one that, eventually, I decided I could step up to. I realised what a great opportunity it was, to try out my own spin on how a shift could be run, that I could bring my own ideas about working culture to that particular team. It gave me more opportunities to use my initiative to help solve local problems. For example, when we helped the local station deal with car crime at a particular pub, we took to staking out the car park in unmarked cars. What resulted was we watched a large drug deal go down. £8,000 worth of cannabis exchanged hands right in front of my eyes, and on my in-car video screen, and we got two men arrested for it. I had never seen such a quantity of drugs; there were eight bars of brown cannabis wrapped in cling film, each of them the size of a medium-sized apple strudel, but I'm sure not quite as tasty!

Another occasion on which I used the "10th man" or "contrarian mind" strategy was during the annual Christmas anti-drink drive campaign. I decided that we would park a plain car and marked car patrol car at a strategic place along the A5 during a night shift, making it look like the unmarked car had been stopped, and the driver was being spoken to. This bit of subterfuge led other motorists, who were a bit drunk and worried about getting caught, the opportunity to turn off the A5 when they saw the blue flashing lights. They found themselves heading down a lane where we had another patrol car parked. It was a clever filter… instead of us doing a load of guesswork, we filtered guilty motorists right into our hands.

I felt fortunate to have found myself with a tight-knit team and a positive manager who allowed me the freedom to use my creativity and initiative, and who granted me the autonomy to make independent decisions. Being given free rein and responsibility at this stage my career, but in an environment where I felt supported and respected, was an essential part of my development. I was allowed to speak up, my superior listened down to me, and so the channel of communication was open and healthy.

I enjoyed these early experiences working in Traffic. I wasn't 100% sure it was my ideal role, but it was certainly preferable to being behind a desk as I joined the police in the first instance to have a direct connection with the general public and because I craved a range of experiences, where no two days would be the same. Having said that, I did know people who'd taken up the desk jobs and they were perfectly happy and thrived. We obviously need both types of personalities to fill all the roles. There would be an unworkable situation if everyone wanted to do the same job. As in all things, balance and individual differences are essential.

CHAPTER SIX:

HOLD MY FIRE

The police in the UK are not usually associated with firearms in the way that they are in many other countries. Within the UK, police officers are not routinely trained and armed but that began to change during my career due to an ever-increasing number of crimes where firearms were used by the criminal fraternity. We now have a higher number of officers trained to use guns and officers who have shown sufficient aptitude with firearms can apply to become an authorised firearms user. In those days, weapons were safely locked away in our vehicles; either behind the rear passenger seats, in the central glove compartment, or behind the front door panels. Only the control room's duty inspector could grant specific permission for them to be removed from those places.

In 1994, when they were beginning to increase the number of traffic patrols trained to carry – covertly, of course – firearms in their vehicles so that they would be ready to mobilise to an incident at a moment's notice, I volunteered to embark upon the training in order to become an armed response officer. The goal was to ensure that each of the three traffic groups in Staffordshire would have an armed response vehicle (ARV) crewed by two authorised firearms officers on duty during each shift, to provide coverage across the county. I didn't dare tell my mother or grandmother!

Embarking on my firearms training was not a decision I took lightly. The ramifications, if called to a scene where firearms were necessary, were huge. The only thing most people know about armed police officers is what they see in films and television dramas, the kind of scene where bank robbers came running out of the bank and armed officers leap into action to stop them. But on the other end of the scale is the situation where a disturbed teenager, drunk or high on drugs, has managed to get possession of their parent's shotgun. Making the right decisions in such situations is a very finely balanced process. I recently looked up statistics on how many potential firearms incidents are averted as a result of officers using their training and communication skills to prevent any firearms being discharged. I was amazed to discover that, for instance, in the 12-month period, March 2019—March 2020, of around 18,000 police firearms operations, a weapon was discharged only on *five* occasions.

Policing is a thankless task for the most part. When you get it right, bad incidents are averted, so no one really notices or expresses much gratitude. However, when things go wrong, the whole world wants to castigate you for it, and it's splashed across the front covers of the newspapers. That's not to say bad policing shouldn't be called out, but there's no harm in thanking police officers from time to time for the work they do that generally goes unnoticed.

*

As with the driver training course I did, I really enjoyed the learning process whilst on the firearms course, and the discipline of being in control of a piece of machinery that carried risk. This was a big responsibility.

The regulation weapon at this time was the Sig Sauer pistol and after we had passed the initial course, we were required to return each month to "re-qualify", to check that we had retained our skills and could use a firearm professionally and appropriately should the occasion ever arise.

On one particular re-qualification session, some twelve months after initially qualifying, we were asked to attempt a new shooting procedure, known as a "detail", at the firing range located on a cold and uninviting unused quarry at Freehay, near Cheadle in Staffordshire. It was during this exercise that I came the closest I ever came in my life to shooting someone!

Six of us were instructed to stand side by side, spaced out at two-metre intervals. We were then told to walk forwards about five metres towards our individual paper targets, turn, and then walk back again to our starting points, ending up with our backs to our targets. When the order came to fire, we were instructed to turn around, reach for our holstered weapon and then fire two shots towards our targets. We practiced the walk a few times and it took a while to get our alignment correct so that we all ended up in a line and not one further behind another when we came back to our starting places. This was critical to avoid someone ending up in the line of fire.

Finally, when we were proficient at getting ourselves back into the aligned position, we were given the order to fire. I turned and fired two times, known as a "double-tap". I was pleased to see I'd hit the target, but less pleased when

I realised one of the trainers was coming towards me shouting and swearing. I could even hear it through my ear defenders. I could immediately see I was in big trouble but had yet to find out what I'd done.

It soon became clear I'd broken a cardinal rule. Although I'd fired at the right time and on target, I had taken my pistol from its holster too early: before I had turned around and was facing my target. The result was, I'd spun around 180 degrees with a loaded weapon in my hand. Putting everyone in range of my weapon, as I spun around, at risk, had my hand slipped. What I should have done was await until I was fully facing my target before taking my pistol from its holster instead of having a loaded weapon in my hand as I spun around, even if it wasn't directly pointing at someone.

The result of this action was that I was not given my firearms "permission" at the end of that session. I'd have to wait another month before re-qualifying. But that moment never came because the incident had stopped me in my tracks and forced me to think about the consequences of what could have happened. This had a profound effect on me, and I had to ask myself some searching questions.

One question that occurred to me suddenly was whether I'd even have time to defend myself if I stopped a motorist who threatened me with a weapon. What were the chances I'd have enough time to retrieve a weapon from a locked section in my vehicle if I was caught unawares like that? During our initial training we were informed that we could decide to "self-arm" without any authorisation being required if we found ourselves in a situation where we believed that there was an imminent risk to life. But I couldn't imagine a situation where the threat would be that high where I would still have time to go and get the weapon from a locked section in the vehicle. And what if the situation ever did escalate to the point where it was necessary to discharge a firearm? What if I was ever forced to shoot someone and I killed them? We were not given any psychological training on how to recover from such a traumatic experience and cope with any mental health repercussions that would no doubt result from such an eventuality. And if I ever did happen to actually shoot and kill someone, what would happen to my family? Would I be harassed by the press? Would I be supported by my employers or would I be suspended or removed from my role? Even prosecuted? This was obviously long before the accidental shooting of Jean Charles de Menezes in the wake of the London bombings in 2005, or the controversial shooting of Mark Duggan that led to the London riots of 2011. My first child, my eldest daughter, had just been born a month before I attended the original firearms course. Was it really fair to her to be adding to the possibility of her losing her father when I was already doing a job that could put my life at risk at any given moment? I quite enjoyed the discipline of firing a weapon at the range, I liked the challenge of hitting a target, but the reality of using a weapon in the line of duty was a very different prospect and I couldn't justify adding to the risk I was already taking by choosing a career in the police force.

With mixed feelings but knowing I was making the right decision for me and my family, I withdrew my position as a firearms officer.

The thought process and rationale I'd engaged with had made me question things that hadn't come up in my training, so I decided to write a lengthy report outlining my concerns. I asked for it to be sent to the chief inspector in charge of the firearms department and, pretty soon after, I was invited to go and see him.

The meeting was ostensibly to check that I was sure about my decision. This in itself gave me even more pause for thought. Who would ever suggest that anyone should be pressurised to remain a firearms officer if they had reservations? Even if there was a shortage of firearms officers, you wouldn't want reluctant ones. This would not be a good look on a coroner's report if it came out that a fatally-wounded police officer had been persuaded to remain a firearms officer after expressing reservations!

I remember the meeting was very congenial. But I also remember how the chief inspector read out each question I'd posed and replied starting with the words, "I would like to think that..." and then he'd express some generalised, theoretical scenario that might happen. This had a two-fold effect on me. One, it convinced me that, with so little real attention paid to the potential risks of what could conceivably happen if things didn't go to plan, I had made the right decision. But, two, it was the first time I'd had serious concerns about the wider training and support that we weren't receiving. There wasn't even a welfare policy in place at that time, to help protect and guide a police officer through what might be one of the most traumatic events of their life.

The conversation did not fill me with confidence and as I left, I confirmed that I stood by my decision to withdraw my service from firearm duties. I never regretted my decision.

I do not know whether things have changed and if firearms officers are now given what I perceive as essential psychological training and support, but I would very much hope that things have changed and there is more awareness of the human and psychological fallout of potential extreme situations.

CHAPTER SEVEN:

TRAGEDY COMES WITH THE JOB... AND WITH LIFE

One of the things my mother didn't warn me about was that bad things do sometimes happen to good people. When I joined the police, I think I had quite a naïve and blinkered view that I'd be engaged entirely with arresting bad people, preventing crime and keeping the vast majority of society safe in their beds at night. What I never anticipated was that there would be occasions when my hours on duty might be spent in the company of perfectly decent, law-abiding families and individuals whose lives had been shattered by tragedies that were largely unavoidable and completely unforeseen.

The first time this stark lesson was to strike me was particularly harsh. This reality check took place on 21st December 1995 – a day burned into my memory.

On this particular day I had been given Stafford to patrol, crewed with a colleague I particularly enjoyed working with. He was logical and level-headed; he always had a fair and friendly manner with members of the public whenever we had cause to speak with them.

Around mid-morning, we experienced, unpredicted – as far as we were aware – by any weather forecasts, a sudden and very heavy snowfall. The sheer volume of snow took everyone by surprise. The snowploughs and gritters hadn't been deployed and operators had to leap into action. As a result, some of the local roads became quite treacherous due to ice and snow. Around three inches of snow had fallen in a short period of time. I was even struggling to control our patrol car and began feeling particularly grateful for all those hours practising on the skid pan in my advanced driver training.

At around 1pm we were unsurprised to receive a radio call to go to the scene of an accident involving a car and a lorry that had collided in the snow. The location was on the A518 as it heads west out of Stafford towards Telford. This was just one of at least thirty road accidents that had been reported that morning.

We got as close as we could to the site of the accident and then trudged through the snow to the exact spot where a 10-tonne "drop side" lorry (one where there is a flat bed and sides that can drop down) had collided with a BMW. The nearside of the BMW had been badly impacted. We could see that a child seat positioned in the middle position of the backseat had been held securely in place by two seatbelts. We were told that the occupants of the BMW, a man and his three-year-old son, had been taken to hospital. The badly shaken driver of the lorry was still at the scene and we drove him to Stafford Police station where we interviewed him. He came across as a very decent and pleasant man who struggled to describe the harrowing events he had just witnessed.

As the investigating officer, it was my job to record any and all evidence I could obtain in order to piece together what had happened. As part of the investigative process, I was going to have to interview the driver of the BMW. The day after the accident, I was informed that his son had been transferred to the City General Hospital in Stoke so I arranged to see him the following day, which I remember was Saturday 23rd December. It was to be the first of many meetings that we would have over the following months.

The initial interview was the most emotional and difficult interview I ever had to conduct in my whole career. I was speaking to a man whose young son's life hung in the balance. He was, understandably, deeply distressed and traumatised. It was a terrible experience asking this man to recall his ordeal, and half way through, we had to cut our conversation short when a nurse appeared asking for his presence at his son's bedside. I had managed to ascertain that he had been driving his son to a nursery school Christmas party on the day of the heavy snowfall.

I arranged to continue the interview after Christmas, on Friday 29th December. The conversation was still extremely difficult as the little boy was not out of critical care and the parents were obviously beside themselves with worry. During the interview, the father asked if I would like to visit his son. We had, by then, established a deeper bond and a familiar rapport so I felt quite honoured to be asked if I'd like to do this.

Nothing could have prepared me for the sight of his little body lying perfectly still in a hospital bed, turned slightly to the right, his eyes closed, hooked up to numerous tubes and wires that were connected to machines monitoring his progress. One thing that struck me was that he looked totally unharmed apart from a white bandage wrapped around the top of his head, as if he was simply sleeping and there was little reason for him to be there. How desperately his parents must have longed to just pick him up and carry him home and put him to sleep in his own bed.

I eventually learnt the course of events that day.

Earlier that day, the mother had set out to drive the little boy to his nursery school's Christmas party that he was eagerly excited to be going to. The nursery school was located in a small village just a few miles west of Stafford. As the driving conditions got worse due to the heavy snowfall, the mother decided to turn back and go home, deeming the journey to be too risky. The little boy was distraught at the thought of missing the party and to be with his friends so his father, who drove a bigger and more robust vehicle – the BMW – decided it was safe to attempt the journey. He navigated the busier urban roads of Stafford without much difficulty, but when he hit the more remote rural roads that were filling up with snow, he started to skid. He lost control of the car, it spun around and crossed over onto the oncoming lane of the single lane carriageway road. This is where the lorry hit the nearside of the car and the little boy's fate was sealed. A true tragedy.

After completing the interview and visiting the child, my colleague and I drove back to Stafford in complete silence. We both had young children and the events of the afternoon had clearly affected us. We couldn't even begin to imagine what the family of that little boy were going through; we didn't want to.

When I got home after my shift ended that day, the first sound I heard was my daughter, who was just 18 months old at the time, playing in the bath that my wife was giving her. I went to say hello to them, watched my little girl laughing and splashing in the water for a few moments, and then went into the lounge and sat down in an armchair. Everything imploded inside me and I started to cry uncontrollably. The tragedy of it all overwhelmed me: the fact that it was no one's fault, that it had been caused by freak bad weather; the timing of the journey; the young age of the little boy; and the fact that it was Christmas. All these things combined and plunged me into a deep grief that it took a while to come out of. This was compounded when I heard the news that, on 2nd January 1996, the little boy lost his fight for life and died of the head injuries he'd suffered in the accident.

In those days, before the police brought in "family liaison officers" to comfort grief-stricken relatives, providing support and comfort to families was all part of the job; an integral part of the investigate process. I made numerous visits to the family in the aftermath, every time doing all I could to offer them comfort and sympathy. As one of the first official people they ever spoke to, and as someone who'd witnessed their little boy in his last days in hospital, I think they felt a closeness to me that helped in some way. My shift sergeant was the "old-school" type who believed you should never get emotionally involved in such situations, or you wouldn't be able to do your job properly. After my experience, I completely disagreed with him. I felt you couldn't do your job properly if you *didn't* get involved on an emotional level.

My inspector was more aligned with me on this point, and was a useful ally to me during this difficult time. He happened to live near the family and even went for a drive with the father to help him get his confidence back behind the wheel.

I was very honoured to be invited, along with members of the ambulance and fire services who'd been at the scene on that fateful day, to attend the little boy's funeral. I couldn't hold back my tears as I watched the tiny coffin carried into the church. That was the first and only time I ever cried in uniform. Again, I couldn't help thinking about the injustice of it all. By then I knew what lovely, good people these parents were. How could such a terrible thing happen to them when there were so many uncaring and unscrupulous people in the world who'd never had to go through such an ordeal? And I thought so deeply about how these people would never get over the tragedy, that the absence of their little boy would haunt them forever.

I was given no official commendation for this work; I didn't want or need one because I was awarded the most precious unofficial one that meant the world to me and was worth more than any awards I could ever have been given. It came in the form of a short letter from the boy's grandparents thanking me for all my support and assistance on behalf of his parents. I have treasured it and kept it safe ever since, along with a small white card from the parents themselves. The front was depicted a dove holding an olive branch in its beak and typed words expressed appreciation for the recipient's kindness and sympathy, stating that the family took comfort in knowing people cared. The card was then signed in blue ink. On my card, the letters "P.T.O." had been written on the bottom of the card, and on the other side there was a hand-written note to me, written in the same blue ink, which simply said,

"Thank you for being here for us – what more can we say."

Every year since that dreadful time, I have received a Christmas card from the family and have sent one back. In the early years, the little boy's name appeared in the card along with his younger sister's name, but eventually his name was replaced by a new child's name. I was glad for them, that they had moved on whilst knowing that their first son would never be forgotten – he would certainly always live in the memories of those of us who were involved with his family at the end of his very short life.

Stepping into the lives of people who are at their most vulnerable, when they have just suffered unimaginable loss, is not easy or pleasant but it can be a real honour to help people in their hour of greatest need. Hand on heart, I can honestly say that this particular tragedy was the greatest police work that I conducted in my whole 30 years' service.

The experience did, however, leave me with this burning question about why "bad things happen to good people" and it wasn't until I read a book much later in life that I began to have a different perspective. The book is even called *When Bad Things Happen to Good People*. The author, Harold S. Kushner, explains why these things happen and why they will keep happening, and the important question is to ask is not why do these things happen but how should we respond to such events, including what we should do next? His advice gave me much to think about and even some solitude when it came time for me to face my own mother's untimely death.

As I am sure many people who have experienced the sudden loss of a loved one will agree, the details of the time leading up to such a traumatic event can become vividly carved in your memory for evermore, as they were for me on Saturday 16th May 1998.

It was already destined to be quite a momentous day for me, in terms of my work, as it was the weekend of the "G8 conference" at Weston Park, Staffordshire and our small force would be stretched to the limit. We had already drafted in additional officers from forces around the country to aid with the security required to protect global leaders and their entourages. All the big guns were due to be in attendance: Bill Clinton, Boris Yeltsin, Jacques Chirac, Helmut Kohl, Tony Blair and countless other dignitaries and delegates.

I had a very early start that day. I drove from home to the station where I was based, from where we were transported to the opulent 17th-century mansion house surrounded by acres of beautifully landscaped grounds. I would be providing support at a security gate on the perimeter of the premises. We had been warned that security teams from various countries sometimes worked undercover to ensure that police were performing the necessary checks before allowing people and vehicles through these checkpoints, so we were all on our toes and following procedure to the letter.

A "port-a-cabin" had been positioned next to the gate where a Staffordshire police inspector would be positioned for the day, manning the phone that had been installed in there and dealing with any issues that arose.

I had been there for a couple of hours when the inspector came to the door of his makeshift office and called me over. I was nervous, worried that I'd done something wrong, that I'd failed to spot a planted imposter from entering. Nothing could have prepared me for what I was told. My mother was in hospital after an accident at home. The control room had tracked me down and I was to leave at once and go to the hospital as her condition was serious.

I was driven back to the station, jumped into my car and drove to Burton District hospital, where she'd been taken, it being the closest hospital to my parents' house. As I raced up the A38 to Burton, I will never forget the moment I finally broke down, listening to a beautiful piece of music called 'The Year of the Dragon' played by the Yorkshire Building Society Brass Band. The middle section of the three parts is particularly moving. It just hit me and I started to cry. To this day, if I hear that piece of music, it affects me deeply.

When I reached the hospital, I was directed to a small clinical waiting area where I found my dad, sitting alone in a terrible state. I was the first to get there to join him. My brother and sister were on their way and joined us shortly after I arrived. I had never seen him like this before, fighting back tears and trembling. I was allowed to go and see my mum and, just like the little boy in the car accident, she looked so peaceful. Even though she was hooked up to a number of machines keeping her alive, she looked as though she was just asleep. I wanted to say, "Wake up, Mum. Let's go home!"

In the waiting room, Dad explained what had happened. She had woken up in the early hours of the morning, feeling unwell, and got out of bed to go downstairs. My dad had told her to wait and he'd come with her, but she went ahead and fell down them; we will never know if she fell because she tripped or fainted, or lost her balance because she was dizzy, but my dad heard a sickening thud as her head hit the wall near the bottom of the stairs. She was unconscious when he got to her seconds later. It's astonishing to think how a split-second decision can so profoundly affect so many lives and cause so much devastation. Decisions that are made every moment of the day. I am sure my dad still wonders "what if?" What if he had moved faster and had got out of bed in time to help Mum down the stairs or if she had just waited a few moments for him to get to her? We will sadly never know.

Eventually we were told that she was going to be transferred to the North Staffs Hospital at Stoke where they would be better able to deal with the massive head injuries she had suffered. We followed the ambulance in stunned silence.

My dad, brother and sister and I set up for a long wait at the hospital. We knew her life was in the balance. Sadly, she passed away the following day. She never regained consciousness. She was only 51.

The doctor who broke the news to us explained that there had been nothing more they could do for her as she had suffered a brain stem injury. In what felt like no time at all, a woman from the NHS donor team came to see us and we agreed, together as a family, that her organs could be donated. We knew she would have wanted that.

We had one last opportunity to say our goodbyes that afternoon before they took her body away.

I miss her every day, even though I often feel her presence with me, especially when I face particularly difficult times (more of which later). My greatest regret is that she never got to meet her eight wonderful grandchildren who, at the time of writing, range in age from 15 to 29. I know she would have been so proud of them all.

CHAPTER EIGHT:

TRAFFIC FROM THE AIR

They say that once you put something "out" into the universe, it never really goes away, and life can have a funny way of returning you to old loves or old unfulfilled ambitions. I had been enjoying my years in the police service so much, I had given little thought to my original dream career, but a seed had been planted that day at school when I watched with envy as my fellow schoolmates were flown around the skies in a Navy helicopter. A strange twist of fate eventually brought me back to my first love: helicopters.

I was on a Sunday afternoon shift at Traffic Support South. Sundays could be very quiet or very dramatic, depending on whether some daredevil motorcyclist decided to test out their skills on quiet roads, or someone who had probably passed the age where they could safely drive had gone for a jaunt around the houses and caused an accident. By far the more dangerous were the speeding motorcyclists on their ever more powerful machines.

I was crewed up with a colleague, we were given the Cannock area to patrol, and we decided to take the laser speed-check device with us. This is a contraption that looks similar to a small video camera that gets set up on a tripod and has a sophisticated way of allowing us to catch unsuspecting speeding motorists from hundreds of yards away. The camera can read a vehicle's speed and rear number plate as it passes. Then there is a choice of following the vehicle and pulling it over, or recording all the relevant details (number plate, time, location, speed, etc.) and getting a fine sent to them through the post.

I remember it was a lovely sunny day and we decided to set up our speed check along the A460 near Hednesford. We had only been there for 30 minutes before we heard what sounded like a high-powered motorcycle screaming up the road towards us. As it zoomed passed us, we discovered it was only a 125cc motorcycle doing an impression of something bigger. The rider wore a helmet but no other protective gear, and where the number plate should have been, there was just a black space. We couldn't get a reading.

It was one of those occasions where we took a tactical decision to do nothing. By the time we'd packed up our equipment, got in our vehicle and attempted to pursue him, he would have been long gone. There was no point. So we chalked it up to a "hope he gets stopped some other way and without harming anyone". As frustrating as it was, we knew we would be chasing our tails by attempting to go after him at that point. We were also fairly sure he'd clocked us and had probably ensured he took a circuitous route home to shake us off had we gone after him, so we were astonished when, a few moments later, we heard the very same high-pitched whine of a motorcycle engine coming towards us, this time from the opposite direction.

We were not going to let this brazen chap get the better of us a second time. We threw our equipment into the back seat, jumped into our patrol car – a new Vauxhall Omega estate, and pulled out just as he whizzed past us. Despite the noise of our siren and our blue flashing lights, the rider did not let up on his speed, he clearly wasn't interested in stopping for a chat. We had a high-speed pursuit on our hands and my colleague broadcast this over the radio to the force control room.

The moment anyone radios in that they are in pursuit of a vehicle – regardless of whether it's a Ferrari or a tractor, everyone in possession of a radio wants to get in on the action. Immediately, we had patrols heading towards us, listening to our commentary in order to work out whether to try to head off the motorcyclist somewhere or join in the convoy behind us. But on this occasion, we had an extra special vehicle join us in pursuit... Air 1, the police force's helicopter, was taking off from its base at Halfpenny Green Airport.

To top it all off, I soon discovered an old friend of mine, who was an advanced driver behind the wheel of a brand new Volvo T5 estate, had been given permission to leave his post on the southern motorway patrol and head towards Cannock to help us.

This was going to be interesting.

We kept the commentary going as best we could but motorcycles always have the advantage of being able to fit through spaces where large estate cars cannot go. The driver also seemed to know the back streets of Hednesford better than us. We had a couple of streaks of luck where we thought we had lost him but caught sight of him again. The commentary from the helicopter was hugely helpful, too, especially when the rider used small passages to escape us. It soon became obvious that we were going to have to use some alternative tactics to get the situation under control. These days, police are trained in something called TPAC (Tactical Pursuit and Containment), which is where you trap the target vehicle that needs to be stopped by boxing it in using a number of police vehicles, but it is not permitted for use on motorcycles as it would be too easy to knock the rider off and they could end up under a police vehicle and potentially fatally injured. However, in those days, we just had to use our best judgement. Sometimes I think society has gone too far and we are denying people – with perfectly good training – their real human agency, the ability to think and judge for themselves. Are we really better off when we follow strict guidelines? Or should we be given more leeway to make decisions based on the individual circumstances we assess in the moment, using our training and innate ability? Surely the "human factor" should count heavily in difficult or high-stakes situations. Yes, we require set parameters within which to operate, but we are not robots; nor should we attempt to become robots – following processes or orders to the letter. We should always think for ourselves in every given situation, assess all factors, and react accordingly. That is the beauty of being human and the value of the idiosyncrasies that we all individually possess. And this is also how we learn. All great innovations begin with an idea, usually one that has been discovered through a particular error or accidental discovery or luck, then built on. We are on a continual journey of building our knowledge and understanding of the complex systems that surround us.

On this particular occasion, our opportunity finally came when the motorcycle turned onto Cannock Road – a fairly wide, straight road. I put my foot down and managed to get past the motorcycle and just in front of its front wheel, giving him no room to get past. I started slowing down and finally forced him to back off. He tried to overtake me on my offside, but Mark was behind and managed to block him in. He had no escape and we gradually brought him to a stop by slowing down. I have a crystal-clear memory of how the rider actually came to a rather graceful halt, sitting upright on his motorcycle but propped up between the rear bumper of my car and the bonnet of Mark's car!

The rider was arrested and taken into custody. We later found out that he was wanted for failing to attend court, and had numerous motoring offences, so it had been worth the hair-raising adrenaline of the afternoon and the slight damage to two police vehicles. But that is not the end of the story for me. In fact, that moment really was the catalyst to the beginning of a whole new chapter for me.

After booking the rogue rider in at Cannock Police Station, we received a call from the air unit to ask if we wanted the video footage covering the pursuit? We did. Next question: did we want it sent through the internal post (known as "snail mail" as it was so slow) or did we want to collect it ourselves that afternoon? As neither my partner nor I had ever visited the air base at Halfpenny Green, we unanimously agreed on the latter option.

When we got to the base at Central Counties Air Operations Unit (the consortium name for the unit serving both

Staffordshire and West Mercia Police, comprising an area of around 2,500 square miles) we met the two police officers and the pilot who'd been aboard the helicopter. The pilot, Alex Candido, was buzzing about having just taken delivery of a brand-new aircraft – the first of its kind in the United Kingdom to be used as a police helicopter. It was a state-of-the-art shiny new "Eurocopter EC135 T1". Alex offered to show us around it.

It was fascinating to see all the latest high-tech aircraft controls, the police camera unit and the "nitesun" torch, a 30 million "candle power" spotlight (candle power is a standard unit of light brightness). The nitesun can be used to illuminate a large area on the ground. From 1,500 feet, for example, it can easily illuminate a football pitch. All the police equipment, the electronics used specifically for police work were housed in a purpose-built box stuck onto the underbelly of the helicopter. This was called the "McPod"; so-called because McAlpine Helicopters in Oxford had built it. With a price tag of £3.5 million, it was an awe-inspiring piece of kit.

With mounting hope, I asked Alex if it would be possible to go for a "spin". He couldn't do it there and then but said it might be possible in a couple of weeks if I booked in. He explained that I'd have to get permission from my supervisor and book in with the duty crew before coming down. He suggested a night shift when the base was generally quieter, in terms of routine tasks to be taken care of.

I secured permission and a date was set. Weather permitting; I was going to fly in a helicopter. I could hardly sleep for the nights in between.

My life was about to change forever.

★

Finally, the appointed time came. I arrived at Halfpenny Green, hardly able to contain my excitement. I was introduced to Barry Flower, the young pilot who would be flying me around. He told me how he'd financed his own flying career. Rather than coming up through the military, which was the more common route, he'd paid for his own training and had flown crew to oil rigs in order to get his experience to the right level. He'd always had his sights set on flying for the police, though, and his enthusiasm for the job was infectious. (It would also later prove expensive, as I was inspired to try to follow in his footsteps!)

I was given a safety briefing, including what to do in the event that we crashed, and then strapped myself into the rearmost seat in the aircraft. I don't know what I'd been expecting but, having flown many times when travelling to holiday destinations, I don't think I realised how different it would feel. Suddenly the two Arrius jet engines were fired up and the rotors above my head started to turn slowly. I tried to keep watching the individual blades spins but this soon became impossible as all four composite blades became a blur. The engine note changed as Barry applied more power through the "collective", a lever in his left hand that looked like a large handbrake. Then, all of a sudden, I was aware we were airborne.

I have no recollection of what task we were actually carrying out. I only remember the feeling of sheer joy as we flew through the night sky, looking down at patches of light illuminating the towns below, interspersed with dark patches that were the woods and fields of the countryside.

In an even more profound way than I'd been inspired to want to work at Traffic Support South after my brief taster working there, I knew this was where I wanted to end up, working with the air support in some way. I yearned to work with machines like the one I was sitting in, and with the people I met on that night shift and when I managed to spend subsequent shifts shadowing them. I was determined to be in the mix when the next vacancies became available at Halfpenny Green.

While I waited for an opening, for someone to leave or retire, I decided to get a jumpstart and took private helicopter lessons at Halfpenny Green in January 2001. The aircraft I cut my teeth in was a Robinson R22 – a far cry from the EC135, but just as exciting to me. This also kept me happy after the sad demise of Traffic Support South.

In April 2000, I had been informed that our Traffic unit was to be disbanded. This happened during the time when I was acting up as sergeant, so it hit me particularly hard. Everyone on the shift and throughout all the Traffic groups was dumfounded by the decision and the repercussions faced as a result of this decision, which we later found out to be a cost-cutting exercise. I was aggrieved that the job I loved and the relationships I'd built with some fantastic colleagues and friends was about to be dismantled. It was soul destroying. I was sure there had to be a better solution. I gave it some serious thought and came up with an alternative plan, which I put down in a detailed report. I focused on why it was not the best idea to disband the Traffic groups as it would lead to higher death rates on the road, lose a vast amount of experience in dealing with road traffic incidents and there would be no passing on these skills to the younger generation of officers coming through the ranks. It would also put officer lives at risk, and they would be forced to deal with serious incidents on fast moving roads without specific training. I could see it was a recipe for disaster on so many levels.

I dropped off the report to headquarters, addressed to the Staffordshire Chief Constable, John Giffard, during a night shift, when I knew that there would be very few people there at that time. I also sent a copy to the Police Federation. I was invited to a meeting with the Chief Constable the following week. I knew this was not an invitation to be taken lightly so I made sure that my shoes were polished and my uniform smart. Would there be tea and biscuits, I wondered?

On the day of the meeting, I was ushered into the Chief Constable's cavernous office. A large conference table dominated the room; his oak desk sat towards the far end of the room. It was seriously impressive.

John Giffard was a very tall, lean man. He had a reputation of being fair and approachable, a totally different character to the previous Chief Constable of Staffordshire, Charles Kelly. I was invited to sit down on one of the conference table seats and the Chief Constable joined me on the same side. He informed me that at first, he had been somewhat annoyed that I had submitted such a report and if I had done it during a previous regime, I would have expected to be sent to police the northernmost backwater of Staffordshire for my remaining career with no hope of ever being promoted.

However, he informed me that I had been courageous and that he was actually pleased I felt confident and safe enough that I could dare write such a report, let alone deliver it. He said that I would not have any sanctions placed on me if I did wish to seek promotion to sergeant. The next twenty minutes were spent with him outlining why the decision had had to be made as the financial position of the force was in a difficult way, with police pensions putting stress on the bank balance. He wasn't obliged to tell me any of this, and my respect for him greatly increased as a result.

The meeting lasted thirty minutes and before it ended, I extended an invitation to him to attend a charity brass band concert at Burton Town Hall in which Derwent Brass were playing with the famous euphonium player, Steven Mead, in aid of the Mayor's Charity. I was the band's secretary at the time. He politely turned down my offer, as diplomatically and firmly as he'd turned down my ideas in the report.

We were finally and fully disbanded in December 2000, after which I stayed on at Lichfield Police Station but was involved in general policing activities as well as traffic support, which was absorbed into the day-to-day duties.

When I think back to this occasion, I reflect on what a good example it is of a time when I spoke up. I may not have succeeded in my objective but because my superior listened to me and consider my points – effectively "listening down" to me – I felt heard and came away from the interaction feeling like I was trusted and respected. My superior had created a psychologically safe environment for me to bring forward my ideas and had respectfully and clearly explained the rationale behind the decision making so that I went away knowing I could trust him to listen to me on future occasions. I had confidence I would be heard, reasoned with and respected. Sadly, this was not always my experience with other superiors during my long career, but it made me conscious of how important this type of interaction is in creating a good working environment and healthy management structure.

*

The opportunity to apply for my dream job as an "Air Observer" finally came in early 2002. I knew that these opportunities didn't come around too often and when they did, dozens applied, so I looked for any advantage I could gain. I had to believe my passion would give me some edge. Not everyone applying would be so deeply passionate about flying, I knew that, for some it was just an opportunity to do something different and get a change from the daily slog of driving a panda car to one incident after the other.

I passed the application stage and found myself at Staffordshire Police Headquarters ready to take the desktop exercises. One was to relate a set of 12 A4 aerial images to an ordnance survey map within a set time. I managed to pass these and found myself invited to RAF Cranwell in Lincolnshire along with the other remaining candidates. The remaining candidates were slowly but surely being whittled down at each stage. I was one of about 15 left. We were to be put through a series of computer-based tests, all conducted in silence, which looked at our psychomotor abilities (camera operation) and our natural ability to deal with multi-tasking and prioritisation. It was a very tense and stressful two hours, but I managed to get through and stay in the race.

Finally, it was time for the actual flight test which involved map reading and an exercise to assess our aptitude for working in a 3-D world: relating what we saw on the map to what we saw on the ground whilst listening to the radio and directing the pilot to a series of pre-planned locations. I will never forget this experience. It took place on 7th February 2002. The pilot I was partnered with was Captain John Caldicott, an ex-Royal Navy Lynx pilot. Memories of my experience at school came flooding back, adding to the adrenaline.

The flying lessons and navigational exercises I'd practiced paid off and I got through to the final stage: an interview.

I did well, but not quite well enough to get the job. As consolation, I was offered a post as "reserve air observer". This meant I would train alongside the full-time observer but would then return to my division after the course. I would eventually be "on call" for when the air unit experienced staff absences for reasons such as sickness, attendance on development courses or annual leave, and I would be invited for further training when opportunities arose. I would also be required to go through the annual Civil Aviation Authority capability tests, known as "line checks".

All was not lost. I still had a foot through the door. With hindsight, I wonder if one of the reasons I wasn't given the permanent role was due to the fact that I'd recently passed my sergeant's exams. The role of Air Observer was constable level. They may have felt that I would be seeking promotion too soon after joining and they'd have to go through the time consuming and expensive recruitment process once again. Or they may also have taken account of the fact that I was learning to fly privately. They might have thought I had set my sights on leaving the police in the not-too-distant future, to pursue a commercial pilot's license.

The two-week Air Observer's basic course took place in March and it was the best course I'd ever completed. Every day brought something new and exciting to learn: navigation, weather, crew resource management, aviation law, fuel checks, dealing with emergencies and more. The map reading skills became more advanced and detailed, and then there was all the high-tech camera equipment to explore, including the Flir (Forward looking infra-red) camera, which was housed in a pod on the nose of the aircraft. This was known as "the all-seeing eye". Another flight test came at the conclusion of the course and I was delighted to be told I'd passed on 11 April 2002.

A week later I reached a personal milestone, an ambition I'd harboured for most of my life, a dream, when I flew a helicopter solo. I had absolutely no warning that it was about to happen.

Even if the only vehicle you've ever been in control of is a regular car, you'll remember that the first moment you get to control it solo is a big deal. The stakes rise dramatically as the size of the vehicle increases, and when it comes to flying, it really is a pulse-racing experience. But every pilot, no matter whether they will go on to be a military fast jet pilot or a transatlantic commercial airline pilot, goes through this experience.

You will be invited to fly solo when your instructor deems you to be ready.

I had been taking privately funded flying lessons with East Midlands Helicopters, who were situated in Costock, a small village near Loughborough, Leicestershire – a 45-minute drive from my home in Uttoxeter. On 17 April 2002, I turned up for an exercise and discovered my regular instructor was away and I was to be instructed that day by the company's Chief Pilot, Glenn Blake as my usual instructor, Matthew Wood, was away on a course.

Glenn and I took off from Costock and flew to Nottingham airport where my training exercise was scheduled to take place. I flew a couple of circuits in a neat and tidy fashion and landed us on the grass steadily. Then Glenn uttered the words I will never forget in his softly spoken Scottish accent.

"Right, I think you're ready to go solo." I wasn't expecting it at that moment, which probably helped as I had no time to anticipate the enormity of the task and get nervous about it. This was the culmination of around four months of training, and all the associated expense. Learning to fly, especially helicopters, is not a cheap affair and it had taken me 36 hours of flying instruction, not to mention the hours of personal theoretical study, to get to this momentous point.

Glenn's endorsement was important. He wouldn't have allowed me to fly solo if he didn't think I was capable. More importantly, he wouldn't have put his company's expensive helicopter at risk. He offered me a few words of encouragement and then got out and stood on the grass in his fluorescent jacket, instructing me to fly the same circuit then land near where he was standing and pick him up. Simple.

I embarked on the most nerve-racking but exhilarating 15 minutes of my life.

Something I hadn't anticipated was the difference in weight I would feel. Glenn must have weighed about 14 stone (around 89 kg) and that's a big weight difference in such a small helicopter. You don't need to apply nearly so much power to take off. But this fact was lost on me at this point. After conducting my pre-take-off routine (checking the wind direction and my immediate surroundings, and radioing for permission to take off), I applied the same amount of power as I had before, shooting into the sky in an ungainly fashion. There was also an adjustment to make in terms of the centre of gravity, which had changed.

I confess, it wasn't the most elegant of take-offs, but I got into the air and suddenly found myself flying the Robinson R22 on my own. I'll never forget the registration was "G-TINK"! I'd done it. I was a pilot! I was flying a helicopter. It suddenly dawned on me that the exercise wasn't finished. I had to land the thing. Was I going to get it down on the ground safely? After completing my circuit of the airfield, I carried out my pre-landing checks, remembering to pull out the all-important carburettor heat stick on the panel in front of me. This prevents ice being formed in the carburettor and causing the engine to stop – not something I ever wished to experience, especially on this of all days! I radioed the airfield tower to let them know a nervous first-time solo pilot was coming in, and then gradually lowered the collective, reduced power and somehow managed to land somewhere near to Glenn.

As with the take-off, the landing was a far from perfect, but we – the machine and I – were suddenly on the ground in one piece and Glenn was congratulating me.

For all the money it cost, and all the adrenaline expended, it was a slight anti-climax to see the one line in my logbook innocuously stating: Ex 12 First Solo ("Exercise 12: first solo flight). But I'd survived and completed it: that was the main thing.

And this wasn't the last I'd see of Glenn. The world of aviation – especially rotary aviation, which is what all aviation related to helicopters is known as – is extremely small and our paths crossed again several years later when he was a training pilot and I was a base manager for NPAS (the National Police Air Service). When stakes are high, as they are in aviation, it's always good to work with people you've had a long-standing working relationship with, where the trust has been consolidated. Trust is built incrementally and evolves over time.

After passing the Police Air Observer's Course in April 2002, I begrudgingly returned to my regular policing duties at Lichfield Police Station. I eagerly awaited the occasional call from the air unit requiring me to fill in as an air observer when they had unscheduled absent staff due to sickness or last minute emergencies (as opposed to annual leave or people off on training courses, which would be planned for and covered by the permanent staff), but these opportunities were few and far between because they had very low absentee rates. If you get the right people in the right roles and create the right working environment, absenteeism tends to be rare. I kept hoping someone might retire and open up a permanent position for me. The situation left me in a quandary. Having passed my sergeant's exams, I was eligible for promotion somewhere, but if I was successful in applying for a sergeant's position, I would probably never get into the air unit again as it would be a demotion. Entry into the air unit as a permanent air observer was only possible at constable level. My dilemma was: should I wait around forever for an opportunity to join the air unit as permanent air observer, spinning my wheels working at Lichfield at constable level, or should I move on and seek a promotion to a sergeant's position somewhere? I could from there hope to get a transfer to the one and only sergeant's position at the air unit, but there would be no telling how long it would take for that position to come up. It could have taken several years, depending on how long the serving sergeant wanted to remain in the post; this was a coveted role and people were never in a hurry to move on from it.

After much deliberation and mixed feelings, I decided to apply for the next round of sergeant boards (the interview process all constables who qualify for promotion by passing their exams have to go through). A new challenge plus the additional salary and pension would certainly be welcome. I was fairly confident I'd be successful because I had, by then, acted up as sergeant for Traffic Support South and also at Lichfield Police Station itself. I had even spent short periods as an acting sergeant at Stoke and Chasetown (a small town just outside Lichfield).

My interview was scheduled for March 2003. Invited to go and see the Chief Constable, John Giffard (for the second time!), I was promoted to the rank of sergeant and immediately posted to Burton Police Station. I was excited to be going back to my home town. Obviously, it wasn't my dream job, but it offered me a fresh challenge yet with some familiar faces. The best part was that I was allowed to continue as the reserve Air Observer at Halfpenny Green, which kept me happy even though the opportunities to fill in were few and far between. I longed to be up in the air regularly working as a permanent member of the air unit.

CHAPTER NINE:

A NEW PERSPECTIVE

The stars finally aligned in late 2005 when it was announced that the incumbent sergeant at Halfpenny Green was due to retire in the November. His official, rather grand-sounding, title was Deputy Unit Executive Officer (DUEO). This was a title given by the CAA (Civil Aviation Authority) but it was a position that had to be occupied by a police officer ranked as sergeant or above. I was the only sergeant in the force who was trained to be an air observer, so things were looking rosy. An additional requirement was that the DUEO had to have completed the Home Office Executive Officers course. Fortunately, I had completed this earlier in the year (so as, in fact, to step in for the DUEO on occasions in my role as reserve air observer, which I was able to do being at sergeant level). They say God works in mysterious ways. Well, this was better than I could have expected. Because I'd had to wait, it had allowed me to complete the qualifications necessary not only to become a permanent air observer without having to jump any more hurdles, but actually to join at a position higher than I would have done if I'd got in originally, two years earlier.

Early in 2005, I had also completed my studies at Staffordshire University and had a Postgraduate Certificate in Management. This had initiated my life-long interest in the study of leadership and management, so I was excited to be placed in a position where I could get more practical experience.

The role of DUEO included overseeing the training of new recruits and the ongoing annual assessment of the current observers. I was also responsible for the Police Air Observers Manual of Guidance, the national document used as a standardized document for all national training of air observers, and ensuring it was kept updated. As part of this process, I was asked to give a speech under the heading, "Training in the UK Environment" at the first ever "Emergency Helicopter Conference" at Olympia. The conference was scheduled for the end of 2005, very soon after I'd begun my role, so I experienced another bout of "imposter syndrome". This was a major aviation conference and exhibition where police air units from all around the world had been invited to attend in order to share new ideas and innovative practices; it was very much an international audience, which didn't help with my anxiety.

We were officially the "Central Counties Air Operations Unit" (CCAOU) and based at Halfpenny Green where we occupied new offices and a purpose-built hangar. I obviously already knew the officers at the base – a total of seven officers from both Staffordshire and West Mercia Police Forces – having worked there as a reserve several times, and I soon settled into my new role. Along with three pilots who were recruits from "PremiAir Aviation" (a pilot recruitment company), we were a close-knit team, which was important when dealing with such expensive equipment and high-risk operations.

I reported directly to the UEO (Unit Executive Officer), Dave Johnson, a retired police inspector who ran the base with huge ambition and pride. We had Dave to thank for the procurement of the new EC135 Eurocopter and the move to the impressive new hangar facility at Halfpenny Green. Over the 10 years I worked with Dave, I believe I learned almost everything valuable there is to know about managing aviation from him.

The final member of our small team, who filled a particularly important role, was Jean Worker. Officially, she was the unit's cleaner; unofficially, she was more like a mother figure to all who came through the unit over the years! She always told us she did the job more for the camaraderie than the money. She was there three mornings a week and never failed to make everyone a coffee and catch up with our news. She was a very special person.

Very early on, I really felt as though I had the best job in the world. I particularly enjoyed the direct responsibility for recruitment as well as developing the training and development staff underwent. I did my own training courses, of course, and became particularly passionate about CRM (Crew Resource Management).

CRM is a mandatory course for all air crew working in aviation. The police must ensure that all their pilots and air observers attend the course once a year, otherwise they cannot legally fly. The course syllabus is broken down into various subject areas such as communication, teamwork, situational awareness, leadership, and accidents and errors. Finding new ways to deliver and make what can be dry subjects more interesting and relatable is a constant challenge. But this is a critical part of ongoing training for anyone working in aviation, as statistics tell us that over 80% of all aviation accidents are caused by human error.

In 2009, I was one of just four trainers from across the country invited to attend the inaugural Crew Resource Management Training course (as in training to become a trainer) to be delivered by CRM aficionados Phil Cottrell and Huw Thomas at Dorset Police Headquarters in Winfrith. Successful graduates of this course were given a Civil Aviation Authority (CAA) licence in CRM training, which gave us the authority to train our colleagues – pilots and police officers – in CRM ourselves.

In the years I'd spent working as a reserve air observer, I had noted that the standard and calibre of officers working in air operations was extremely high. This was a result of the high competition for roles. Working on the air unit was very niche and thus sought after, so when vacancies did arise the number and quality of applicants was exceptional. The level of responsibility when working on the air unit exceeded what a constable would normally be expected to shoulder. Often officers would be directing a pursuit, providing advice to a commander on the ground, or guiding search teams to a missing person. These roles often involved taking life-or-death decisions.

I soon became accustomed to the looks of amazement on people's faces when I told them what I was doing at this point in my career. I realised how easy it was for us, in the air unit, to become almost blasé about the work. I believe some of this is because when you are dealing with situations that are so critical, when lives hang in the balance, you can't remain aware of the enormity of that in the moment. You have to get on with the job and put aside the dramatic nature of the situation. Only when you have a moment to reflect later on, when the emergency has been dealt with, does the full impact of what you've been involved with hit you. Indeed, sometimes you don't even realise the danger you've put yourself in when these situations arise. I remember one such occasion that my great friend and colleague, Ian Worthington – who was sergeant at the North Midlands Air Support Unit at Ripley, Derbyshire at the time – was involved with.

In July 2007, the North Midlands Air Unit received a report that a member of the public had sighted an elderly woman floating down the River Derwent in Derby. Ian, along with PC Graham Fish and pilot Eric Church, answered the call and flew to the area where the woman had been sighted. They soon located the woman, who appeared to be in her early 70s and was wearing pyjamas and a cardigan.

From the helicopter, the crew attempted to throw a buoyancy aid to the woman, but their efforts were unsuccessful. Aware that there was a large weir and sluice gates downstream, they concluded that they were under enormous time pressure. They decided that the only thing they could do if they wanted to save the woman from drowning was to jump from the aircraft and into the fast-flowing River Derwent.

With very little time to think through what they were doing, Ian and Graham jumped into the river and somehow managed to get the woman to the riverbank, where they waited until a small boat commandeered by local fire service came to rescue her.

Telling the story, Ian explained that it may have been a dangerous choice for them, but the only other option was to watch the woman drown in front of their eyes. For him and his team, it wasn't a choice; they at least had to exhaust every possibility rather than simply watch the woman perish. What they did was truly heroic, but they would say it was their instinct in the line of duty.

I have seen so many police officers on so many occasions think in exactly these terms. I think it must be hard to understand if you've never been in such a life-or-death situation, but we take an oath when we join the police service, to do whatever we can to preserve life, and so it's not much of a dilemma.

One of the most dangerous tasks we had to undertake in the air unit was casualty evacuation (CASEVAC). Invariably, this would take place at night. During the day, air ambulances would usually perform this task, but they are not authorised to land at ad hoc sites at night so if casualties had to be evacuated to hospitals at night, police helicopters have to step in and perform the task. Police helicopters have special dispensation from the CAA to do this and have the necessary specialist equipment. A powerful lamp strapped to the underside of the aircraft helps the crew to assess a landing site for any dangerous wires or obstacles, and a thermal camera can detect the location of a body in the dark even if it's obscured – for example, trapped under a car.

We only carried out CASEVAC in life-or-death situations, where medical staff were present and could advise, and when there was no other means to transfer the casualty to a hospital. For us, we would generally be transferring the injured to the North Staffs Royal Infirmary (NSRI) or the Selly Oak Hospital in Birmingham. Both were designated trauma centres and had illuminated helipads.

There were always a number of intricate and urgent decisions to be made. If we were called to a CASEVAC situation while we were still on the ground at the unit base (as opposed to being in the air en route to or from another mission) we would leave a crew member behind, making the rear observer's seat available for the paramedic or doctor who was at the scene and would be accompanying the seriously injured casualty to hospital to help keep them alive on the journey.

On average, we would receive about one CASEVAC request per month.

Performing a CASEVAC task was a real rite of passage for any new observer. As it would only be the observer and the pilot in the aircraft, the observer would be managing several systems at once: the camera, the nitesun (that 30 million candlepower spotlight) and the radio, while simultaneously navigating, and keeping both the police control room and the hospital constantly updated. It was a huge test of training and mental focus to perform all of this while someone's life was hanging in the balance.

I will never forget my first CASEVAC as a crew member. We were on the ground at base when we received a call to attend the scene of a car crash in which a woman had received life-threatening injuries. After the aircraft was swiftly reconfigured to make the space for the stretcher, I accompanied the pilot, my good friend Barry Flower, to the scene. We had to land in a field five miles south of Uttoxeter. The woman was in a critical condition, which wasn't surprising seeing as her car had literally been severed into two pieces. We managed to get her to the hospital in an impressively short space of time, but we later learnt that she hadn't survived. Sadly, these situations are always touch-and-go. The casualties are usually in such a critical state that their lives hang in the balance; there is no guarantee they will survive. It is always a huge rush of relief when you discover that someone did survive thanks to your efforts.

Another CASEVAC call that will remain indelibly printed on my memory also involved Barry at the controls. This time, another police officer, Chris Hollis, and I were accompanying him to a call to look for a person who had been struck by a train in Shropshire. A local train driver had reported that someone darted in front of his train as he was headed south towards Shrewsbury. We were called out to help search for the body. A number of police patrols were already on the ground, and another train was being driven down the track slowly in order to help with the search, which was compounded by the fact that it was at night.

Eventually a female body was found – still alive – but was badly injured and missing a large portion of her arm. Our mission turned to finding the missing arm!

The severed body part was eventually located under the slow-moving train that had been involved in the search.

We were asked to transfer the woman and her detached arm to the hospital. It was a rural area so it didn't take long to find a convenient field to land in after checking carefully checking for electricity pylons or other obstacles and wires.

I went to speak to the medical staff as Chris and Barry got the aircraft prepared for loading up the casualty. I will never forget one of the paramedics coming over to me and saying, "I've put the woman's arm on the front seat of the helicopter; it's in a plastic bag." Not a sentence you hear every day!

I then returned to the helicopter and when I looked at the front seat, the bag wasn't there. I quickly asked Chris if he'd seen it. He said he'd moved a plastic bag to the back; he'd assumed it was some of the paramedic's equipment. When I informed him of the bag's true contents, he went pale and looked a bit queasy.

Miraculously, the woman and her arm arrived at the hospital and the arm was reattached to her body. However, it transpired that she had been attempting to end her life when she ran in front of the train, so she was going to need more help than physical care. I remained hopeful that she also got the psychological help she needed. As I hoped for all the many suicidal cases we encountered.

One such incident involved the tactical use of the aircraft itself. In April 2014, a crew was asked to search for a man who had threatened to take his own life. He was believed to be in the Tipton area of Birmingham, and it was believed that he had the means to set fire to himself, that this was his dramatic strategy to end his own life.

The team on that occasion comprised Capt. Jamie Thomsett, PC Chris Hollis and PC Gavin Jones. They managed to locate the at-risk individual and directed officers on the ground and an ambulance crew to where he was. During this time, the officers on the ground valiantly attempted to talk him out of harming himself. Unfortunately, he couldn't be dissuaded and proceeded to pour flammable liquid over himself and set fire to his body. Despite the horror they were witnessing, as the flames engulfed the man, the team in the air took decisive and swift action. The pilot positioned himself directly over the man and used the downdraft of the aircraft's rotors to put out the flames. They managed to extinguish the flames and the man was rushed to hospital when the ambulance arrived, having sustained serious burns. As with many incidents we attended, we never found out whether the individual survived the horrific injuries he sustained. We have no idea what happened to him but at least he was given a chance.

Throughout my time there, I marvelled at the selfless actions of the crews at Central Counties Air Operations Unit.

Decisions in a life-or-death situation do not always, necessarily, involve some dramatic or selfless act of heroism. Sometimes they are simply a decision to follow a certain routine course of action.

I remember one occasion well that occurred in May 2011. I was the front seat tactical flight officer that day, and my colleague, PC Paul Packwood was in the rear commander's seat. Our pilot was Capt. Dave Mawson. Dave was a highly skilled pilot with a great personality, so it was always an enjoyable experience to fly with him. He was also shorter than average and had particularly youthful looks, which he made up for with bags of confidence. The unit had given him the playful nickname of "UNMIN", which is an airline abbreviation for "unaccompanied minor". We joked that his crew were, in effect, his two guardians accompanying this minor when he went flying.

On this particular occasion, we had been tasked to search for a volatile and dangerous male missing from the town of Halesowen in the West Midlands. The man had mental-health issues and was suffering from depression.

He was also armed with several high-powered weapons and was threatening to use them on his family, who lived in the West Mercia Police area, and on any police officers if they confronted him.

We were all acutely aware of the potential seriousness of the situation, particularly in light of an incident that had happened a year before, when a similarly armed person had been on the run in Northumbria, and this had led to a seven-day manhunt during which two people had been killed, and a police officer had been shot in the head. This officer ended up blinded from the wound and sadly later took his own life because he was unable to live with his disability.

A "Gold, Silver and Bronze" command structure was initiated, which highlighted the level of concern surrounding the incident. Only major incidents warranted this. It is where very senior officers are brought on duty comprising the Gold "strategic" level, then one level down, the "Silver" team will work out the tactical decisions, and then the "Bronze" team carries out the operations. Given that it was the Sunday of a bank holiday weekend, it would have been very expensive to bring in the additional resources, so this is an indication of how seriously that they were taking the threat. This is a good example of the importance of flexibility in allocating resources. It's impossible to budget for exactly when serious incidents are going to take place, so it's vital to factor in enough contingency to cover all eventualities, whenever and how they happen.

Paul and I gathered snippets of intelligence throughout the day and we got airborne a few times in order to search for vehicles that we knew the man had access to. Using our combined experience and Paul's local knowledge of the Wyre Forest, we agreed on where best to utilise the aircraft with the incident commander; eventually we were successful in finding the suspect's vehicle parked in a secluded car park. Observing the vehicle from a safe height and distance, using the aircraft's camera, we were able to guide the firearms officers to the scene. They soon located the man and arrested him without a single shot being fired or anyone being harmed. All we had done was provide the situational awareness, which allowed the senior officers and firearms officers all the information they needed to make the best decisions. Fatalities were averted simply by following a fairly routine course of action.

Paul, Dave and I all received a "Quality Achiever Award" for our efforts. Our certificates stated, *"This award is presented for your professionalism and tenacity and for taking the leading role in the strategic direction in an operation which had a positive outcome."*

On a more light-hearted note, I was once admonished by the head zoo-keeper at Dudley Zoo.

In May 2010, we were flying over Dudley monitoring a group of English Defence League (EDL) protesters who had taken up residence on the rooftop of a disused building in the heart of the town. After many hours of negotiation, the West Midlands Police commanding officer decided that enough was enough and called for the protesters to be forcibly removed. They were going to send in the trained public order officers. Our part of this cunning plan was to create a visual distraction, along with a lot of noise. This was one thing that we very good at!

To create the overall distraction, we came down as low as we legally could on the opposite side of the building to where the public order officers were going to approach from. It worked perfectly and the dispute came to an abrupt but rather impressive conclusion. The public order officers broke through an adjoining slate roof and appeared directly in front of the protesters, taking them by surprise. Our noise had provided the cover for dozens of officers to smash their way through the slates on the roof.

After the initial "shock and awe" tactic had been played out, I received a radio message from the duty inspector in the control room asking me to phone him immediately using the aircraft's radio system. He wanted to speak on a private line and not on the operational channel. As I was occupying the rear seat in the aircraft, I made the call. I feared the worst. What on earth had we done?

Well, it was a conversation and request that I had never previously had or am likely ever to have again. The inspector explained that he had received a phone call from the head zoo-keeper at the nearby Dudley Zoo and he was not best pleased by our low flying and presence that day. He had asked that we fly higher as we were disturbing the lions and giraffes.

Fortunately, the operation was wrapping up and our part in it was pretty much over. We monitored the final moments of the police operation from a greater height before returning to base. I did find myself wondering if police in the Serengeti game reserve received similar requests to fly higher lest they disturb the giraffes and lions!

The first few years as the DUEO of the CCAOU flew by (pardon the pun) and involved a lot of "settling in". This included all the training courses I undertook and the building of key relationships. As well as my immediate team, I had to get to know aircraft engineers, visiting pilots, other air base managers and aircraft maintenance suppliers. And every day brought something new to learn about the quirky nuances of the aviation world.

At this point in time, the Air Operations Units around the country were owned by individual polices forces; each one an autonomous and individually financed operation. Some bases were strategically placed at airports, others were positioned at force headquarters to reduce running costs as it was expensive to rent land at the airports. We were in regular communication with each other, swapping notes on various issues we encountered, and I particularly enjoyed going to the national trainers' meetings that were attended by police air units from across the country including the Irish police (The Garda). The meetings were always well supported with trainers from all around the country converging to discuss training issues and attempt to standardize training methods across the whole country. I had to take note of any changes to the training methodology that were made during these meetings and ensure that they were reflected in the Police Air Observers Manual of Guidance. These twice-yearly meetings were always enjoyable and came with the added bonus of the competitive streak that set in, with each successive host police force trying to outdo the efforts of the previous one in terms of standards of accommodation. Eventually it was the turn of The Garda to host and I thoroughly enjoyed my first trip to Dublin and being put up in a particularly luxurious hotel.

International travel seemed to be one of the new perks of the job and I suddenly had opportunities to visit places I'd never imagined travelling to before – one of those destinations being Jamaica.

CHAPTER TEN:

FLYING FURTHER AFIELD

The UK's FCO (Foreign and Commonwealth Office) had negotiated an agreement to assist Jamaica tackle the illegal drugs and gun smuggling occurring in the Caribbean. This involved bringing members of the JDF (Jamaican Defence Force) to the UK to train with the British Army, and reciprocally sending members of the British Army to train with the JDF in Jamaica. I had the great fortune of becoming involved with them through a fairly tenuous link.

The JDF had taken ownership of two new Bell 407 helicopters. These were donated by the US in an effort to address the popular smuggling route between Cuba and the US run via high-powered speedboats. The Bell 407s were fitted with thermal cameras, supplied and built by a company called FLIR (Forward-looking infra-red). These cameras with their powerful lenses allowed us to see events unfold from a several miles away both in daylight and night-time conditions; these were an updated version of the cameras we used on our aircraft.

My invitation was something of a fluke really. A West Mercia police officer on secondment to the FCO was asked for a recommendation for the best person to help train the JDF to use the Bell 407s effectively. He suggested Ian Edgington, a long-standing member of CCAOU at Halfpenny Green. Ian jumped at the chance to fly off to Jamaica for a couple of weeks and suggested he take me along as I had the relevant CRM Trainer qualifications and could conduct a full review and analysis of their training needs. We would also be working with the Jamaican police force the JCF (Jamaica Constabulary Force).

The first hurdle we discovered was that the JDF and the JCF were not on the best of terms. The JDF didn't trust the JCF, believing the police force to be corrupt and involved in underhand dealings on the island. They basically accused them of being involved in the drug problems they were attempting to tackle. There was a lot of friction between the two organisations, and as teamwork is critical when working with such complex, expensive and powerful machines such as helicopters, it was vital that we found a way to bring them together as we trained them. Teamwork is essential in most jobs but within aviation, and specifically police and military aviation, it can more often mean the difference between life and death, because the risks increase as the stakes rise.

On arriving in Jamaica, we had the opportunity to do a little sightseeing and get an insight into local history and culture. I was immediately struck by the fact we were staying next door to the hotel where Bob Woolmer, the former English cricketer, had died the previous year when he'd been visiting in his role as coach to the Pakistani cricket team during the world cup. His death had led to much speculation in Jamaica, back in England, and in the cricketing community. Initially assumed to be a heart attack, a coroner's report suggested malice, and evidence of death by strangulation. A murder investigation was opened and eventually closed without any charges being made. A later inquest resulted in an "open verdict", meaning that foul play could not be ruled out. There were rumours that it was a gang-related murder.

I was a little unnerved to discover how high the murder rate was in Kingston. It was estimated there was one murder every six hours! Most of these took place in the garrisons, which were enclaves loyal to one of the two competing political parties in Jamaica. A hostile turf war existed between these constituencies, fuelled by the warring political factions that emerged after Jamaica secured independence in the 1940s. One of the worst areas for crime was the Tivoli Gardens area. Even the police were reluctant to get involved there. We had a security briefing from someone at the British Embassy before we set off exploring. So we knew which were no-go areas without an official escort. But the places we did explore were absolutely beautiful. There is so much natural countryside on the island, and of course, stunning beaches to relax on.

By the time we started the first of the two four-day courses a few days later, we had a good basic grasp of the local political and social conflicts. We hoped our exercises would help break down the barriers between the JDF and JCF and build stronger relationships between them. They would need those if they wanted to make the best use of their new kit. We spent time trying to understand their ways of working, to see if we could help them improve and streamline these. They operated differently from how we did in the UK in that the JDF were entirely responsible for the piloting and maintenance of the aircraft, and also supplied a crew member in addition to the pilot. The JCF would then supply one additional officer to complete a three-strong crew and provide police knowledge over the scene of an incident.

They had a very long-winded method of calling for aircraft assistance at police led incidents. If the police wanted helicopter support, the police control room had to make the request to the duty officer who then had to send the request through virtually every police rank to a chief officer who was the only person authorised to approve the request for the use of a helicopter. If the helicopter support was approved, the JCF would call JDF where the request had to be pushed through more layers of bureaucracy until it reached a senior officer at the airbase to see if there was availability to complete the request. Only then could the police put the call out to their trained observers to see who was available to drive to the army camp and join the helicopter crew. The whole process could take up to an hour, by which time the opportunity for helicopter involvement to make a difference to the incident had probably been wasted. So their aircraft were really only of use in pre-planned tasks as any opportunity to use them proactively was scuppered by red tape.

We found all this quite astonishing and it made us appreciate the fantastic procedural efficiency we were able to work with in the UK. I was very keen to pass on some of that experience, to help the Jamaicans understand how rapidly the chances of success diminish with every wasted second not having the helicopter in the air once the need for it was established.

We had an even number of JDF and JCF staff on each of our courses: four men from each organisation. The first exercise I tasked them with was a simple problem-solving exercise using several sets of children's coloured wooden building blocks. We split them into pairs, ensuing there was one JDF officer and one JCF officer in each pairing and then gave them instructions. They sat back-to-back and one member of the team built a structure that the other member couldn't see. He then instructed his teammate to build an identical structure simply using verbal instructions. At the end of the exercise, we would see how alike the two structures were.

We did this in turns so that everyone could watch each pair do their best and worst. Playing devil's advocate, we ensured one of the pairings included a high-ranking JCF inspector with a low-ranking JDF private. This was fascinating to watch. The superintendent built a structure first and then tried to explain it to his teammate. We watched the whole exercise go from bad to worse and ultimately fail spectacularly, but it was a great opportunity to show our course members what had gone wrong. The exercise involves a huge amount of level-ground communication between the participants. Because the JDF officer was of a much lower rank, he never questioned the JCF inspector's instructions. The latter never checked in with his technical subordinate to ensure the instructions were clear enough. This exercise is so simple but so vital. It literally exemplifies the core message of this book: speak up to those ostensibly placed in authority over you; listen down to those technically in much lower ranks to you. When it comes to communication, you cannot afford to have anything but clear, open and free-flowing channels. Decision-making needs hierarchy but communication should be unfettered by rank.

Ian and I took turns flying in the aircraft alongside the pilot with one member of JDF and one member of the JCF completing the crew. The rest of the students split into two groups, one playing the roles of the "police" and the other playing the "criminals". It was like an airborne game of hide and seek conducted at night to see if we could "capture" the students using the thermal camera. This carried more risk than I'd bargained for. I was aware that the vast army camp we were based at bordered some of the garrison townships of Kingston, but I didn't realise the danger that put us in. After we took off and completed a circuit of the camp, Ian radioed to ask the pilot to illuminate the aircraft lights so that those on the ground could see where we were. If we'd been in the UK, we would have had red, green and white positional lights blazing, along with bright white anti-collision strobe lights so he was unnerved by not being able to see us. I made the request to the pilot, who immediately said no.

In fact, his words were, "No, or they will shoot at us." I didn't think there was any point in repeating the request!

Once we were back on the ground, we questioned the pilot, explaining that it would be completely illegal to fly without the mandatory lights displayed in the UK. We wouldn't dream of doing it. He explained that any aircraft lights seen over a Kingston garrison would be regarded as a target and we would likely have found ourselves the targets of gunmen. The crews had already had experience of bullets hitting the aircraft on previous occasions. This was a bit of experience we were unlikely to have gained in our regular duties in the UK!

The Jamaica visit was a huge success. We were even presented with a small plaque celebrating our visit and a beautifully embroidered JCF badge. To this day, I have kept in contact with the JDF crew trainers. We regularly swap information and training notes.

One of the most important lessons I learnt in life, that I have always applied to training, and try to impress on those I teach to train, is one I picked up quite early on in life when I was playing in the Derby-based brass band, Derwent Brass. We were a very competitive amateur band and entered numerous competitions. We were being led by world-class trumpeter and guest conductor, Richard Evans. We were rehearsing a particularly difficult piece at one rehearsal, in preparation for a competition. I was really struggling to keep up. Finally, after several attempts we got it right. But this wasn't good enough for Richard. He spoke the following words, which I have never forgotten and tried to live by: "You shouldn't be rehearsing until you get it right, but until you cannot get it wrong." That one comment changed my whole philosophy on training and practice.

I was extremely happy in my role as Deputy Unit Executive Officer (DUEO). I enjoyed managing a motivated, passionate and high-performing team and got a lot of job satisfaction from the fascinating nuances the world of aviation brought to it. I even liked the slight detachment from direct policing. It was actually very refreshing to not have to deal with the command-and-control police ethos on a daily basis as the role exposed me to people outside of policing.

Police air support is a good example of where there is a necessary fusion between public and private sectors. The nature of this relationship always brings advantages and disadvantages. We had to have a close working relationship with big private companies such as McAlpine Helicopters, Flir, Eurocopter and Airbus Helicopters. These are private profit-driven companies, but we were performing a public service and were funded by the taxpayer. This is a similar relationship to the one the NHS is required to have with the pharmaceutical and medical device industry. This is a relationship that has long intrigued me. How can you have a private company, focused on profit margins, working ethically and transparently with police air support, an organisation purely focused on public service? It's a strange juxtaposition and a very delicate balance. I'm not sure there is an easy answer.

(Indeed, in July 2018, I was asked to deliver a presentation to the Continuous Improvement Meeting – previously known as the Police Eurocopter User Group – in Oxford. My presentation brief was to provide the assembled delegates, from both Eurocopter and the National Police Air Service, with a base manager's perspective of running a police air base, drawing from my experiences at Halfpenny Green and latterly Lippits Hill. I used it as an opportunity to put a direct question to the delegates, asking: *"How does a public organisation form a synergy with a private commercial company? In essence, how does a non-profit community focused organisation (NPAS) work with a private, profit focused company (Airbus)?"*)

*

In October 2008, a unique opportunity presented itself to me. I spotted an advert in a monthly helicopter magazine. Bristows, one of the largest helicopter companies in the world, was on a recruitment drive. They were offering apprenticeships to wannabe pilots, offering applicants training to fly their large Eurocopter Puma helicopters to oil rigs in the North Sea, after which you could further your training and learn to fly air ambulance helicopters all over the country. A company like Bristows often paid for already-qualified pilots to be trained on specific aircraft or instruments, but it was rare for them to offer apprenticeships to people with little or no flight training. They would pay £70,000 of the one-year £100,000 training course based in Florida, so you could have to invest £30,000 of your own money, but the advantage was becoming bonded to a company like Bristows. You would be pretty much set for life.

After much deliberation and some serious conversations with my wife, I decided to apply for it. I saw it as a win-win situation. If unsuccessful, I would remain in a fantastic job that I loved. If successful, I would finally fulfil my dream of becoming a helicopter pilot. If I didn't at least try, I was sure I would regret it.

I obviously said something right on the application form because I was invited to Oxford Air Training at Kidlington Airport to attempt the computer-based assessment, similar to the one I'd done at RAF Cranwell but geared more towards potential civilian pilots hoping to train as commercial airline pilots. As I awaited my turn, I noted how much older I must have been than the other applicants. I was only 41 but most of them looked like they were fresh out of school or college. I wondered if my life experience, especially my policing experience, would make me a better candidate for helicopter pilot school than any of them. Or maybe my age would stand against me as they might get less return on their investment. Being older does make you more prone to illness and injury, which could result in the loss of your licence. I also wondered if, because we carry more "baggage" as we get older, we become harder to train in core skills. This is probably why it is generally much easier to teach a child how to play a new musical instrument than it is to teach an adult.

Whether or not my age had anything to do with it, my new career was not to be as I failed the computer assessment. By now I was beginning to accept that my dreams of being a helicopter pilot were probably not going to materialise. But this is a good life lesson. Not everyone has the talents and abilities that line up with their ambitions. There must be many disappointed wannabe astronauts in the world! Sometimes you have to accept that you don't have the necessary skills and aptitude for your dream job. That's okay. Just find something to do that brings you as close as you can get to it. Like I did! I was disappointed but glad I'd given it a go, and more than happy to carry on with the job I so deeply enjoyed. Although there was a big bump in the road on the horizon before 2008 came to a close.

On the afternoon of Thursday 4 December 2008, I was attending a Police Air Support conference at Warwick University when I got an urgent call from base to inform me of an incident. At the time, our UEO, Dave Johnson was on extended leave visiting family in Australia, so I was filling his shoes and the buck stopped with me, so to speak. I was told, on the phone, that our aircraft had made a heavy landing at West Mercia police headquarters. Thankfully the crew had not been injured but they were badly shaken up as something had obviously gone drastically wrong. They sensed they had been just seconds from serious injury and even death.

When I hung up, I immediately shared the story with a fellow conference attendee and DUEO from the East Midlands Air Support Unit. He suggested I inform the Air Accident Investigation Branch immediately since the accident involved the potential loss of life or loss of the aircraft. I was grateful for the advice as it was the first time I had ever dealt with such a serious incident involving a threat to the lives of our crew. I contacted the AAIB directly and they were more than willing to attend to investigate what had caused the problem.

I left Warwick and headed straight to the West Mercia base at Hindlip Hall to speak to the crew and examine the damage to the aircraft.

I was told they'd been in the air over Worcester and had been in the air for around 50 minutes before the aircraft began to experience a very unusual vibration. If this happens when you're driving, you can immediately pull over and stop. It's a little more alarming when you are airborne. Hindlip Hall, the West Mercia Police Head Quarters, was their closest landing site. They were almost on the ground when there was a loud bang, which sounded like metal on metal, followed by repetitive banging and heavy vibration. They were still about three feet from the ground. The pilot announced an "emergency shutdown" which involves switching everything off immediately and telling everyone to jump out and run to a safe location.

The crew evacuated, the helicopter landed heavily and, thankfully, nothing caught fire. Fire is always a huge risk in a helicopter as there are so many moving parts, electronics and a lot of fuel moving around at extremely high pressure.

Once the four main rotor blades had come to a halt and they were sure nothing was on fire, the crew took a closer look at the aircraft to try to establish what had gone wrong. It transpired that one of the two scissor link mechanisms in the aircraft had become detached. These are vital parts in any helicopter as they are involved in the positioning of the rotor blades and help the pilot direct the aircraft. Fortunately, the EC135 is fitted with two rather than the single mechanism you would find in most aircraft. A simple nut-and-bolt system holds a scissor link in place, and the nut is secured by a simple split pin, which is about the size of a child's hair clip. On close inspection the crew discovered that the split pin and nut were missing. The bolt had obviously been kept in place for a while by centrifugal forces when the rotor blades were spinning but had come completely dislodged as power reduced on landing. It was obvious that the split pin hadn't been replaced and the nut had come loose.

It is astonishing to think that a tiny piece of metal worth pennies is so essential to the running of a multimillion-pound aircraft and its absence could lead to the total destruction of such a machine.

Ongoing discussion about the incident also revealed that there was a contributing factor that could have made the whole situation much worse. The pilot flying that day was shortly due to be going through a regular pilot competency check where his autorotation skills would be tested, so he was considering practicing his autorotation skills on this flight. Thankfully, for some reason, he decided not to practice his autorotation skills. If he had gone ahead and the autorotation practice had taken place 3,000 feet above Worcester, I am not at all confident that the crew and aircraft would have survived the loss of one of the scissor links. The forces involved and the loose flailing metal component would have potentially caused untold damage to the aircraft's key controls and it would likely have become uncontrollable and crashed.

The advantage of working within a small, close-knit team is that ability to discuss even the most life-threatening incidents with honesty and transparency. We had created an environment of openness and psychological safety, so the crew were able to talk through their experiences with each other and other members of the unit, without feeling guilt or anger.

We had to wait until the following day for the AAIB inspector to arrive and assess the aircraft. One very pertinent piece of information was that the helicopter had only just been returned to us after an extended period of unscheduled maintenance at Eurocopter to investigate a vibration in the aircraft's rotor blade mast. If the incident was in any way related, Eurocopter would shoulder a very heavy responsibility for returning the aircraft before ensuring it was absolutely safe. And it became very obvious that they suspected culpability when someone in their customer service team became quite angry that we'd involved the AAIB, saying they could have dealt with it themselves. This made me even more certain I'd done the right thing by calling the AAIB (Air Accident Investigation Branch).

As the administration of this incident unfolded, I became ever more convinced that Eurocopter would have tried to cover up internal issues if the AAIB hadn't been involved and wouldn't have opened an internal investigation, as they were forced to do. Obviously, they were nervous. If word got out that they'd almost destroyed a helicopter and killed an entire crew simply because someone hadn't checked a split pin was in place, and hadn't investigated or taken responsibility for it, it would have cost them millions in sales and maintenance, and possibly damaged their reputation for a long time. As it was, the repair cost them £120,000 so it was a very expensive lesson.

The reports from the AAIB (which can be accessed by the general public – filed under "Reference 1/2010") and Eurocopter were subsequently published and summarised the causation factors as to why the accident occurred as well as provided a long list of safety actions and recommendations that should be put in place in order to avoid such a travesty happening again. The AAIB report really shone a light on exactly how astonishing it was that something as small and cheap as a split pin being missing could have caused such a dangerous accident that could have destroyed an aircraft, not to mention the lives of the three crew members.

Accidents like this, and worse, do occur and are usually the result of a number of small decisions or mistakes or factors all adding up to the perfect storm. In other words, they are rarely the result of one single human act or a single malfunction. There is generally a whole list of little events, mishaps, oversights, assumptions, poor decision-making, as well as a lack of training or established poor practice that come together to cause disaster. But at any point somebody could step in and become a barrier to further risk, preventing those disastrous and ever-increasing links in the chain accumulating. In aviation and CRM, that "perfect storm" scenario is often referred to as the "Swiss Cheese Model".

This is where all of the holes in slices of Swiss cheese line up so that you can see from one side of the cheese to the other and it's through that combined hole that the huge disaster takes place.

You will see this whole process take place time and time again in documentaries such as those made by National Geographic Air Crash Investigation.

There were 12 specific recommendations made in the AAIB report that centred on communication within the maintenance team at Eurocopter. There had been a verbal handover between maintenance crews and that had led to a misunderstanding about the status of the aircraft. This could have been avoided with a fully documented handover. The exact nature of what had to be done was not communicated properly, and that meant that the position of the aircraft in the hangar also caused a problem because the engineers were unaware that they needed to spin the rotor blades through a full 360 degrees turn to check the relevant parts had been replaced. This all led to the absence of the split pin going undetected. What compounded this was the fact that, while two certified engineers were charged with carrying out safety checks, as they also supervised the hangar, they were often distracted by numerous phone calls from customers and other engineers. As a direct result of this report, going forward, all engineers performing safety checks were required to wear red tabards to signify they were carrying out such duties and were not to be distracted or interrupted. They also created a rule that no mobile phones were allowed in the hangar area. These seem like small details but they may well have created the environment that led to future lives being saved.

A whole raft of training recommendations came out of these reports and I used my own personal experiences of the incident in my CRM sessions as I could give detailed examples of the importance of so many factors of CRM.

The reality of the potential dangers of flying helicopters was really brought home to me through this experience. I was reminded of the critical need to focus on safety and to ensure that no details are missed. Many people think that a large-scale disaster will never happen to them but there are never any guarantees. No matter what you do to reduce risk and check all details, the ultimate flaw may be out of your control.

In recent years, I have been doing extensive research into how human beings tick. I've been looking into risk assessment from the point of view of our human strengths and weaknesses. When I consider the AAIB recommendations in this context, I can see that a a vitally important element is missing from the report. It does not address the potential failures and weakness in the leadership and management that may have contributed to the event. All of the recommendations were aimed at correcting "shop floor" actions with none directed at the management. The report did not seek to analyse and question the systems and processes put in place by management that created the environment that the engineers worked in. Were the engineers who took the flak for the failures identified actually compromised by the working environment they were unwittingly subjected to? Were they in a state of burnout, perhaps? Were they asked to do things above their competence level? Furthermore, were the managers themselves compromised by being in positions that they were unsuited to? Had they been over promoted? What external factors were working on them? Perhaps they were experiencing detrimental circumstances in their home lives that impacted on their working competency.

Going one step even further, were the people who conducted the internal Eurocopter investigation the best people for the job? Or were they subjected to any internal or external factors that might have compromised them? You could certainly say they were acting with specific bias because they were working for the company that was under investigation. This is the regulators regulating the regulators.

The independent AAIB should have gone deeper.

CHAPTER ELEVEN:

AIR OPERATIONS UNIT IDENTITY CRISIS

When the police service was hit by financial cuts as a result of the Conservative—Liberal Democrat coalition government austerity policies, air units were the first to come under financial scrutiny. I was reminded, at the time, of the saying that bureaucrats see the "cost of everything and the value of nothing". Here was a great example. How could you weigh up the cost of running an operation against the value of saving someone's life? Why could no one see the big picture and calculate that even a few cuts in just one area could massively reduce the value of the service we could provide?

While CCAOU survived the worst of the cost cutting thanks to a restructuring process, unfortunately the restructuring was done in the worst possible way. The senior leaders charged with the restructuring did not seem to understand the very first principle of change management, that the most important aspect to consider is the value of each individual member of staff: people are the fundamental building blocks upon which every organisation is built. You cannot get people engaged in any process of change if they cannot picture how they are going to be part of that process, and how it will affect them personally. As a result of this most basic oversight, leaders lost positive engagement with the very staff who could have driven positive change. Change was imposed on them and this created a disengaged workforce, which in turn led to conflict that manifested in many different ways.

I watched this downward spiral happen in real time. The experience was a negative one, as it was a case of a faceless authority on high meddling with the lives of individuals of whom they had no specific knowledge. We had a really good, functioning collection of autonomous, well-run air support units across the country. They were stripped of their individual identity and team pride when they were brought under central control without a proper consultation process. If the big brass at the top of the hierarchy had taken the time to talk to individuals, to get to know them and ask their opinions, things could have been very different, and we could have ended up with a much more positive outcome. They made no attempt to "listen down", so no one had the opportunity to "speak up".

The restructuring process started in April 2011 when the CCAOU was merged with three other Midlands air bases under the management umbrella of the Central Motorway Police Group (CMPG). We were to become known as the Central Region Air Support Unit (CRASU). At this juncture, at least we kept our identity, but I grew concerned when I proposed sharing some of the unique methodology and techniques we had developed as a unit with the whole group and my suggestions were ignored. That was a small red flag that was to grow into something that really gnawed at me. Some of those techniques included ways of finding missing persons in fewer flying hours; involving a combination of more specialised staff training, increased control-room awareness and better liaison with specialist search-trained officers. It seemed counterproductive, and even quite immoral, to dismiss them. But this was my first taste of centralised bureaucracy that serves the careers of authoritarians rather than improve the true efficacy of operations. People were speaking up but no one above them was listening down!

Next step on the road to the homogenisation of our operations was worse. This was the abolition of all the regional groups in favour of a national organisation. More centralisation. By the end of 2013 we had been annexed into the "National Police Air Service" (NPAS). We were to be "hosted" by the leadership and management structure of West Yorkshire Police force from its HQ in Wakefield. The idea that a unit operating, say, in the South West of England was to report to someone in Wakefield, spelled nothing but disaster to me.

Rather than resulting from a well-considered, logical consultation process (which I very much doubt would have concluded that we needed a top-down managed national air support unit), NPAS was created simply as the result of a cost-cutting exercise.

★

I was very proud of the people I worked with when, despite the unpopular and disruptive changes, our culture of great teamwork and camaraderie endured. Nothing could have provided better proof of this than our sudden deployment to Glasgow in the wake of the Clutha pub incident in November 2013.

I was at home on the night of 29 November 2013 when I heard on the news that there had been a helicopter crash in Glasgow. I immediately had an uneasy feeling – call it a sixth sense – that the crash involved a police helicopter as very few helicopters operate at night, especially over built-up areas. I was soon to learn that it was the very same make and model as our aircraft at Halfpenny Green: the EC135. I was distraught to hear that all three occupants of the helicopter had been killed and there were deaths amongst the multiple casualties who'd been hit on the ground.

Throughout the following day, my team and I made numerous phone calls to establish whether our EC135 helicopter was going to be grounded. This is often the case in these circumstances. Until the cause of the crash can be established, it is assumed that there could be a system malfunction or design flaw on the aircraft. We had to check if the worldwide fleet of EC135s were to be grounded. It was confirmed eventually that the fleet was not to be grounded but that, if any crew member felt uncomfortable flying in an EC135, they were not required to for a period of time. As a unit, we all confirmed our decision to continue to fly our aircraft.

I actually worked a night shift that very night, barely 24 hours after the tragedy in Glasgow. When we found ourselves hovering over a public house in a built-up area of Birmingham searching for a burglar, my mind wandered and I was gripped with thoughts of what the crew of the Police Scotland aircraft must have gone through the previous night.

The loss of the crew and aircraft reverberated through police aviation and hung over each one of us like a very dark cloud. It brought home how dangerous this strange job I was doing was and how quickly your life can be extinguished.

The following week, I was asked to assemble a team of our staff members to head up to Scotland to provide support to Police Scotland. I initially thought I might struggle to get volunteers since it was a big ask for people to abandon their own families only days before Christmas and head up to Scotland for an indefinite period of time. To make matters worse we would be flying over the area where the crash had occurred, and in the same aircraft type that, only a week before, had crashed killing all on board. I imagined it would be difficult for everyone involved in the decision, especially for the family members and loved ones who would remain at home, undoubtedly worrying. All too often, we forget about the ripple effect of our decisions and actions on the people we love.

As things panned out, however, I actually experienced more issues dealing with the *disappointment* of officers who had desperately wanted to travel to Scotland to assist their colleagues, on the unit and in Scotland, but we didn't have room to take. I had a set number of staff members that would be required to resource the aircraft for the shifts that needed covering.

On Friday 6th December 2013, we travelled north to Prestwick Airport, which was around 40 miles south west of Glasgow. We were to be based at Royal Naval search and rescue air station, RNAS Gannet, and we were well looked after. There is a definite camaraderie within the world of aviation and the helicopter community is an even smaller, and thus more intimate, family within aviation. As our Naval hosts flew search and rescue missions in some of the most difficult terrain and hostile conditions imaginable, I am sure they felt our pain of losing colleagues in such a tragic way. Our role was to assist Police Scotland in any way that we could, answering the calls that our Scottish colleagues would have ordinarily answered.

Our presence in Scotland was essential as we were one of only two teams in the country, at that time, trained and equipped with night-vision goggles, which made it safer for us to operate over unfamiliar and demanding terrain. I was immensely proud of my whole team, who were happy to spend the next two weeks in Glasgow, away from their friends and family in the pre-Christmas period, helping out. This was a real testament to the environment of support and teamwork in the wider police air support community. Even though it was unnerving to hover over this scene of devastation, when only days before, a similar aircraft had plummeted out of the sky onto the buildings below, it was an honour to help out at such a time of crisis.

Being hosted by the Royal Naval base also had an upside as, when we were given a day off on the Sunday, they asked if we'd like to take part in one of their regular training sessions, which would involve being winched into one of their distinctive grey and red Sea King helicopters and going for a "spin" around the local area. We jumped at the opportunity.

We were all given a safety briefing by the crew. All seemed fine and as I was being winched into the Sea King,

I looked up at the aircraft to see the beaming face of the Lieutenant Commander looking down at me from the open doorway with his right hand on the wire and left hand on the controls, but moments before I reached the top, he stopped the winch motor and left me dangling there like a maggot on a fishing line. I stared at him, startled. He kept smiling at me and finally said, "That's for the speeding fine." I suddenly remembered talking to him days before and mentioning I had worked in the police traffic section before joining the air unit. He'd told me he'd received a speeding ticket a few months previously, whilst driving up from the south west of England to Scotland.

He didn't leave me there too long, just long enough to feel he'd had his sweet revenge on the British Police for his speeding fine. I was soon relieved to hear the renewed motion of the winch and feel the increased pressure under my armpits. I was hauled into the aircraft and guided towards one of the very basic cloth seats, where I sat waiting while the other five of my fellow crew members were eventually winched up.

We had a very pleasant flight over Prestwick, Troon and Ayr and the surrounding area. It was a beautiful sunny and crisp day and I was even allowed to sit with my feet out of the door. I took some stunning photographs. We discovered, too, that the flight was preparation for their forthcoming Christmas visits to local schools where they would hover in the air until the children saw them, and then winch down a crew member who was dressed as Santa Claus. He would then collect a sack of letters to Santa from the children. This was a bit of a public relations exercise to say thank you to the community for putting up with noisy helicopters flying over their homes at all times of the day and night, usually as they flew off to rescue people stranded in the Irish Sea.

We persevered in the new culture under NPAS but in April 2015, the base received the devastating news that the Halfpenny Green base would be closed in December of that year, as a result of a strategic review conducted by senior officers at NPAS. They had decided that even more cost-cutting was needed, and they had to reduce the number of air bases in the Midlands. West Midlands police force would keep their base at Birmingham Airport and cover the areas previously covered by Staffordshire and West Mercia Police forces. I knew this meant that those areas would get very little coverage and I was appalled that such a decision could be made without consideration for the potential cost to life.

I decided to write a report to the West Yorkshire Police superintendent who had conducted the review. The report gave a very detailed and logical argument as to why Halfpenny Green should remain. My recommendation was to close the base at Birmingham International airport and instead to cover England's second largest city from Halfpenny Green and Husbands Bosworth in South Leicestershire. That way, we could provide a service to forces across the Midlands as well as into parts of Wales. We were also a much cheaper unit to run, not having the expensive costs of a rental at a major international airport to consider. We had our own purpose-built hangar and office facilities at Halfpenny Green.

I received a simple, short reply thanking me for my report but informing me that the plan to close Halfpenny Green would go ahead and operations would be centralised at Birmingham International. I will never forget the deep disappointment I felt. Not even a conversation, just a "no thanks, your opinion is not needed" type of reaction. This was exactly the type of stonewalling that was to continue to haunt me for the next few years as I battled to be heard in an environment that was increasingly closing down debate.

In the end, Halfpenny Green closed as an operational base some months earlier than December. As is often the case when any major change involving the closing of a base or organisation is happening, employees do not simply wait for the date of closure before looking for ongoing work, they will proactively commence their job search as soon as they know that their post will be coming to an end. We knew that if the pilots left us, we'd be babysitting an aircraft that was not going anywhere. In the end, due to lack of pilots, our helicopter was redeployed elsewhere, and we were closed down earlier than planned.

I was offered a job as one of three base managers at Lippitts Hill, an NPAS base serving London. I wouldn't have minded so much if it hadn't been such a huge commute, involving having to spend several nights a week away from home. As a consolation, I would be working with the Metropolitan Police Force and I was excited by the prospect of that opportunity.

CHAPTER TWELVE:

A BIRD'S EYE VIEW OF LONDON

In the final months of 2015, I took time to prepare myself for the move to Lippitts Hill before taking up my post there at the beginning of January 2016. I got a taste of my new 142-mile round trip commute to Essex. If I left at 4.30am and had a clear run, I would arrive sometime between 7.30—8.00am. I got familiar with the base, including visiting the accommodation block where I'd be sleeping a few nights a week. And I scheduled times to fly over London – both during the day and at night, which was, quite literally – night and day! The capital looks entirely different from the air lit up at night than it does in the day, like two different worlds.

Set a few miles north of Loughton within Epping Forest, Lippitts Hill was originally used as an anti-aircraft emplacement site to shoot down German bombers as they navigated their way towards London using the huge Lea Valley reservoirs as locating points. It was later used as a prisoner-of-war camp for captured German soldiers. Most of the buildings dated back to the Second World War and had hardly been updated since those times. The Metropolitan Police acquired the site in the 1960s and had developed it for firearms training and some specialist units, including the air unit. Two large hangars and a concrete helipad had been built, and a grassed landing strip had been created in a nearby field.

The accommodation block was cold and basic. The standalone shed had a dormitory area where a couple of large wardrobes acted as dividers between five single beds. The heating was rarely on and the communal washroom housed a low-pressure shower that gave out a drizzle of water (warm on a good day) but at least they had the good sense not to ask for any rent from the pilots who used it by night and day when they had too short a break between shifts to go home.

The twelve-hour shifts required us to work four days on and four days off. I would generally work Monday to Thursday or Tuesday to Friday, with flexibility if I was required to work during a special event or a night shift. I often worked longer than the designated twelve-hour shift and would end up in the staff canteen before or after shifts, talking with whoever else was there. That was the hub of my social life on the nights I was sleeping at base.

There was a fair amount of tension in the air amongst staff members, most of whom had not been best pleased with the NPAS takeover in October 2015. They had been perfectly happy being the Met's own dedicated air support unit and this structural change had ruffled feathers. I did my best to get to know them and listen to their grievances without comment to begin with. I needed to gain their trust and show my support.

★

My first few months at Lippitts Hill were to be a real baptism of fire as we prepared for the visit of the President of the United States, Barack Obama, and his wife, Michelle, who were scheduled to arrive in the UK in the April. This was a huge learning curve for me as I had never been involved in such a large-scale operation before. The air support would be playing a huge part in his protection as he flew into and out of Stansted airport, and between all of venues where he was due to attend various events during his presidential visit. I was grateful to be surrounded by people who had been involved in large-scale planning before so I could watch and learn, which I thoroughly enjoyed.

Two weeks before the scheduled visit, I was asked to attend a meeting with the CAA (Civil Aviation Authority) at their London offices in Holborn, hosted by the Head of Airspace. The meeting was attended by representatives from Heathrow Airport, Her Majesty's Household and Marine-1, the US Marine Corps who were responsible for all the flying arrangements for the President. They handle the giant Sikorsky helicopters often shown on TV taking off or landing in front of the White House.

We were all assembled for the meeting with the noticeable absence of the Marine-1 team. They arrived late and walked in like characters from *Top Gun*, three men and one woman, smartly dressed in tailored suits with expensive-looking sunglasses tucked into their top jacket pockets. They were the advance team, responsible for all the pre-planning in advance of the President's arrival, ensuring that everything was timed to perfection with no detail forgotten or overlooked.

We were informed that we would be leading the air package with one of our EC145s, which would accompany the Presidential helicopter on its flight from Stansted to London. It would be landing at Winfield House, the London home of the US Ambassador, where the Obamas would be staying during their visit. This impressive residence is located on the edge of Regent's Park and backs onto London Zoo. We were told it was essential for us to lead the convoy because the American pilots flying the President's aircraft were unfamiliar with London and since the airspace was so busy over the UK's capital (with flights taking off and landing at both London City Airport and Heathrow regularly), we needed to keep them on a tightly controlled flight path.

After the meeting, one of my colleagues suggested we take the marines to a local pub. Once they had beers in hand, they relaxed a bit. We got to know them better and learnt more about how Marine-1 operated, which was fascinating. In return, we were able to give the Americans a British history lesson and unique experience. My colleague, Capt. John Roberts, had a connection at the Tower of London, a man known as "Billy the Beefeater" and got us all an invitation to watch the historic "Ceremony of the Keys" – a 700-year-old ritual conducted at precisely 9.53pm each night in which the main gates of the Tower of London are locked. It has only been missed once in its entire history; one night when the warders were knocked off their feet when a bomb landed nearby during an air raid in World War II.

It led to a very memorable evening. This group of two air unit staff, a member of the CAA (Civil Aviation Authority) and four US marines ended up being given a private guided tour of the tower by "Billy the Beefeater". He explained the history of the Beefeaters and how this was the colloquial name given for the monarch's official guards responsible for the security of the Tower of London and showed us the historic keys that had been used for centuries to lock up the Crown Jewels every night. We were invited to view his private quarters, where he showed us all the different uniforms he had to wear depending on the occasion and the duties required of him. The Americans took it in turns to try on the red scarlet tunics and to hold the Beefeaters' ceremonial spike, photographing each other to memorialise this unique opportunity. At one point I went to use Billy's bathroom and found myself looking out at the most spectacular sight. Tower Bridge, all lit up, was mere yards from the window. I had to pinch myself; how had I ended up here? A Staffordshire police officer going to the loo overlooking one of the most iconic landmarks in the world.

The "Ceremony of the Keys" took place in mere minutes but was quite spectacular to witness. The guard's division marching over the cobbled stones in their heavy boots, wearing their great coats and black busbies (the very tall fluffy-looking hats), and the warders barking out their orders into the cold night air. I knew none of us would ever forget it and I kept replaying the whole day in my head as we made our way back to Lippitts Hill.

A week before the Obama's official visit, we conducted a rehearsal with the Marine-1 aircraft to ensure that all elements of the air package knew what they were doing and where they were going. I got a front row seat in the rear aircraft; we were taking two in total. It was a bright sunny day; a great day for flying. Although we were mindful of the fact that "on the day" our task would be carried out at night, so conditions would be more challenging.

We began by flying to RAF Mildenhall in Suffolk – the base of the American air force – where we were taken to a briefing room and given all the particulars for the route. When we returned to our aircraft, we were part of the full convoy lined up in the airfield. There were three "Osprey" aircraft ahead of us. These remarkable machines are a sort of hybrid between a plane and a helicopter. Much larger and therefore able to carry more passengers than a helicopter, they have the advantage over a plane in being able to take off and land vertically, so no runway is needed.

We flew to Stansted to familiarise the crews with where they would land and wait for the Obamas to come through the "Harrods" VIP terminal. Then our entourage flew on to Winfield House and from there on to Windsor Castle where the Obamas would be joining HM the Queen for tea. We were informed that only one of the Ospreys was permitted to land at Windsor Castle as the engines scorched the grass terribly as they took off and landed, and HM was not having them destroy her entire lawn!

On the way back to RAF Mildenhall we were joined by a US Marine Corps Sikorsky Black Hawk as we flew across London taking in views of the new American Embassy in Battersea, and The Shard near London Bridge.

The rehearsal had been exciting enough but on the "real" day I managed to get upgraded to the lead aircraft where I was one of a crew of three plus a passenger, a member of the US Secret Service, who was to travel with us at all times during the three-day trip. She was a very serious, stern woman but we chipped away at her rigid veneer and soon had her if not laughing at least smiling at our quirky British police humour.

The three days thankfully went smoothly without a hitch. I was quite mesmerised the first time I set eyes on the sheer scale of the entourage awaiting the President's arrival at Stansted. The place was packed with Secret Service officials, dignitaries, police, members of the press, and an endless array of vehicles, including the President's limousine that was there on standby at all times in case there was an issue with the aircraft or weather prevented us from flying. But I soon got used to the numbers of people involved in this extraordinary event. And I still feel very privileged to have experienced it.

Another unforgettable experience I had during my time at Lippitts Hill, but one that could not have been more different in nature from a Presidential visit, was my first exposure to the Notting Hill Carnival. On this occasion, I would not be in the air but underground, based at The Metropolitan Police's Special Operations Room (SOR) at Lambeth. This underground control room was built for the Olympics in 2012 and has since been used for major events where large number of different units and departments have to come together and coordinate operations.

For the officers in the Metropolitan Police, the Notting Hill Carnival was a well-known event. For me, it was a whole new world and – I was to discover – a far cry from any of the village fetes I'd attended in my life.

I was given the opportunity to get a first-hand "on the ground" experience on the Sunday afternoon and driven from the SOR in Lambeth up to Notting Hill to meet the chief inspector I was to shadow, just one of thousands of police officers in attendance. I was immediately struck by the sheer mass of people, many with brightly painted faces, some in costumes covered with glitter and jewels. The atmosphere was electric. People were in great spirits as the Sunday is traditionally the "family day" so there were a huge number of children in the parade and the crowds. I had never experienced anything like it. The combined sound from all the sound systems on the vehicles and static stages caused my whole body to vibrate. And I'll never forget the delicious aromas of jerk chicken and other traditional foods being cooked emanating from the Caribbean food stalls.

After a walk around the carnival, we ended up at a school that had been commandeered as a rest area and central base for the police on the ground. I had a coffee and chatted to some of the officers before being driven back to the SOR in Lambeth where I re-joined the team coordinating all the communication throughout the event using command-and-control computers, radio systems and a video feed, which enabled us to monitor the event from a number of CCTV cameras dotted around the Carnival.

Our job during these two intense days was to be the liaison between the event commanders and provide specialist advice on how best to deploy and manage the helicopters if and when necessary. We had two aircraft dedicated to the Carnival that were in the air more or less constantly from 10am on the Sunday until 2am on the following Tuesday morning. This required a really intricate team effort to manage the flying hours and maintenance schedules.

Every two hours or so, a meeting was convened to get a situational report about what was going well and where any hotspots of potential crime were. As well as the police, these meetings were attended by representatives from the London Fire Brigade, the London Ambulance Service and

Transport for London. They all fed in their own reports to the event commander. How the commander computed all of the information coming in and built the mental picture in order to make critical decisions was mind-blowing.

During those two days there were 25 stabbings, some life-threatening. They tended to be gang-related and the Carnival simply served as an event where these gang members knew their rivals would convene. The violence wasn't related to the Carnival itself. And I got a sense of how critical our role had been when the commander announced that the two-day event had been deemed a success because "no one died"!

Wednesday 22nd March 2017 started out like any normal day but it soon proved to be far from any normal day and became more surreal and traumatic as the day progressed.

Ironically (as would become apparent as the day unfolded), we were on a maritime counter terrorism exercise at the Royal Marines base in Poole, Dorset, on the south coast of England. Terrorist attacks can occur at sea as well as on land and they are responded to by the Special Boat Service (SBS), which is a division of the Special Forces. The hijacking of the Nave Andromeda off the coast of the Isle of Wight in October 2020 was an example of an incident where the SBS intervened and de-escalated the situation so that no one was hurt, and the hijackers were taken into custody.

The Lippitts Hill police air support unit often have a role to play in such operations, having the training, the endurance and camera technology to provide the "eyes in the sky" for military special forces in the event they are required to board a vessel and bring a threatening situation under control. Our unit was one of the very few air units within the UK at that time that regularly trained for the ditching of an aircraft in water, so we had the legal aviation credentials to be allowed to work out to sea. Crucially, we had all been trained in HUET (Helicopter Underwater Escape Training). Helicopters have an unfortunate tendency of turning upside down if they crash into water because the majority of the weight of the aircraft – the engine, the gearbox and rotors – are all situated above the fuselage. People trapped in a submerged helicopter have tragically and needlessly died when they become disorientated in the darkness and swim towards the roof, not realising they are swimming *away* from the surface and into deeper water. A prerequisite for all crew members staff conducting helicopter operations over water was having undertaken the HUET training.

HUET training is an unforgettable experience. Mine took place at a training facility in Fleetwood near Blackpool. We were kitted out with wet suit, crash and buoyancy aids and instructed to sit in a metal capsule that simulated the interior of a helicopter fuselage. The capsule was ceremoniously "dunked" three times into a very deep but bespoke swimming pool: the first time, we were submerged into the water, but the capsule did not roll over; the second time, we had to push a window out from its frame before escaping through it. The third and final time (and, for me, by far the worst) was when the capsule dropped into the water then turned over 180 degrees before we needed to escape again through the window. This one was horrendous; I panicked and unbuckled my harness early, getting through the tiny window and pushing myself to the safety of the surface, before the capsule had stopped turning. I burst through into the air, gasping and gulping air into my lungs, like a submarine conducting an emergency surfacing exercise. The instructors asked me to repeat the exercise as I'd "escaped" too early, but I flatly refused. I thankfully passed the course and – to date – have thankfully never experienced this particular form of torture again.

My role in the scenario we were practising that day in Poole, was to man the exercise control room and form the link between the senior Special Forces officer and the aircraft somewhere out at sea. I had performed this exercise once before, but I was no less daunted at the prospect.

We were all set to start that afternoon when word came through that there had been a serious incident on Westminster Bridge, and we needed to get the aircraft and our crew back to London urgently. In those first few moments, all we knew was that something very serious had happened, but we couldn't get any specific detail. One report stated that a car had gone into the Thames. But we soon discovered that it was a suspected terrorist attack, and eventually got the chilling news that a police officer had been stabbed and badly injured. After instructing the aircraft and crew to get airborne and head north, I jumped in the car with my good friend and colleague, Sgt Andy Hutchinson, and we high-tailed it back to London. We had been asked to report to the Special Operations Room in Lambeth, the very same room I'd been introduced to during the Notting Hill Carnival. A major incident had been declared and would be run from the SOR.

Speeding up the M3 with a blue strobe light attached to the unmarked car we'd driven to Poole in, more reports started to come through. And, before long, we were aware that a number of people had been killed, along with PC Keith Palmer.

We weaved our way through London and made it to the north side of Lambeth Bridge, which had been closed to all civilian traffic. We identified ourselves to the police patrols and were allowed to continue over Lambeth Bridge to the south side where we parked up outside the SOR. It was quite eerie to see the area completely deserted apart from a few police vehicles. In the basement at Lambeth, we were given the full update as to what had happened and we discussed how best to deploy the aircraft for the duration of the day and the following day.

There was something very sombre but very serious and almost reverent in the atmosphere that day, a steely resolve that our work was for our late colleague. I had never met Keith, never worked with him, never knew his circumstances or what kind of man he was, but I felt connected to him because of the often unspoken agreement that the police are one family, and in the same way that you would always go that extra mile for your own family, when something happens to a fellow police officer, no matter which police force they are from, it ups the ante.

I was off duty and at home on Monday 10th April, the day of PC Keith Palmer's funeral with full police honours at Southwark Cathedral. I was sent a very short clip of our aircraft as it hovered for a moment close to HMS Belfast and London Bridge before taking a coordinated bow (a dip of the aircraft's nose) and then conducting a fly-past of the cortege as it entered the cathedral. It was so simple but effective, poignant and meaningful, and I found myself moved to tears. Perhaps it was the cumulative stress that I'd experienced on the day of his murder, two weeks previously, that had caught up with me and made me more emotional than usual.

The final incident I must mention that occurred during my time at Lippitts Hill was, of course, that terrible fire at Grenfell Tower. I came on duty during the morning of the incident and was briefed on how our crews had been working through the night, and what dreadful scenes they had faced. Their role was to provide the scene commanders with imagery of the incident so they could make informed decisions as to how to tackle the fire. It is impossible to imagine exactly how the crews felt as they witnessed the escalating situation whilst hovering over the scene. They had a bird's eye view of the inferno and as they moved around the building capturing video footage through the aircraft's powerful thermal camera, they saw people perish in front of their very eyes. Such horrendous sights can never be unseen.

In the media in the aftermath, there was some criticism levelled at the air unit. People were frustrated and angry that they had not done more to save lives, like land on the roof and try to recue residents. This is an understandable feeling, but it is unrealistic. There was no way to land a helicopter on a burning roof. Other critics said that it was cruel to fly helicopters around the building as they may have given trapped residents false hope. But, again, they miss the big picture. In an incident like this, there are so many different forces and elements involved, but all are working together desperately hard to reduce as much death and destruction as possible. If you only look at one element, you can't know what specific job they have been tasked with that may be essential to another, more hands-on, part of the operation. There is always more strategy involved than you could imagine in high-risk and high-stakes situations, and if one team member was to deviate from instructions for a moment, it could have a knock-on effect with terrible consequences. When split-second life-or-death decisions need to be made, everyone has to work as a team and with a very organised structure of command. This is one occasion where the "command-and-control" structure has to kick in for the duration of the incident. Even in this situation, we have to have a working environment and a culture of psychological safety so that a junior team member would feel confident and comfortable enough to speak up if they identified a critical problem.

I was very happy at Lippitts Hill. There was rarely a dull moment and I was proud to be a member of the world-famous Metropolitan Police, second only perhaps to the New York Police Department in terms of familiarity for the general public. However, 2019 brought events that completely shattered my world and career.

CHAPTER THIRTEEN:

A TOXIC ENDING AND NEW BEGINNINGS

The majority of my duties as a unit base manager at Lippitts Hill involved the running of the air base in terms of managing the crew and operational requirements relating to our equipment. But there were a couple of occasions on which I was asked to perform functions, that I can only describe as political or bureaucratic, which sat very badly with me, and sent my career on a downward spiral that I just couldn't recover from.

In 2018, NPAS took a decision to close our Boreham air base; the crew and aircraft would be transferred to Lippitts Hill. I was asked to ensure this information did not become public knowledge until the transfer had been completed. This felt wrong to me.

We already had a sensitive and volatile relationship with the locals. The air base was surrounded by residential homes, and those residents were understandably not keen to have their peace and quiet disturbed by police helicopters taking off and landing. They were well informed regarding all their rights, and the requirements for take-off and landing procedures that were designed to reduce noise and disturbance. We would get angry letters or phone calls the minute any of these were broken especially if a visiting aircraft deviated from the designated flight paths, in and out of Lippitts Hill. It was very obvious to me that there would be an outcry if the local residents heard that we were going to have additional aircraft and crew using Lippitts Hill. Furthermore, I predicted that the locals and their councillors would quickly work out that they had been kept in the dark about the transfer and all hell would break loose.

I contacted the NPAS communications team in West Yorkshire suggesting that we formulate a proactive communications strategy with local residents, pointing out that failure to do so might well breach our internal "Code of Ethics", that stated we had to promote openness and transparency, and to exhibit honesty and integrity at all times. I was shocked by the response I got. I was reprimanded for "challenging" the integrity of a junior member of staff (someone in the Comms team) and informed that I would be debriefed by the Flight Operations Director and a negative personal record entry would be made on my file. This all seemed unjustly harsh when I was simply attempting to fend off any future conflict with local residents and councillors. I certainly hadn't made any personal remarks about the integrity of a member of the Communications team.

Thankfully no long-term damage had been caused to the good relationship – one that had been created with hard work, understanding and diplomacy – we had with the residents of Lippitts Hill.

The next time I was asked to yield to a plan that jarred with me was when a decision was made to change the work patterns of the 17 NPAS base managers across the country. This time, I better understood the reasoning behind the decision but I vehemently disagreed with it and could see numerous problems unfolding as a result of it.

Until early 2018, we had enjoyed a flexible work pattern. There was an informal, but perfectly effective, agreement that base managers would step up and cover for each other at a moment's notice if necessary. Central command in West Yorkshire had decided that this would be replaced with a formal and rigid system. I knew immediately that this would undermine the loyalty and goodwill that base managers had traditionally shown to each other. On a practical level, the changes would involve a new shift pattern that felt completely unworkable. It would involve working 8am—4pm on seven consecutive days, then around three days off, and then back on for that run of seven days again.

I canvassed the views of my fellow base managers and 6 out of the 17 told me that they would likely leave the service. This would mean a huge loss of experience along with the additional costs of recruitment and training new staff. The costs could easily run into hundreds of thousands of pounds. So it couldn't possibly be justified by being classed as a cost-cutting exercise.

When I finally got to the bottom of what had motivated the decision, I could understand it, on a superficial level. It had been noticed that, in the previous 12 months (since March 2018), NPAS had received requests on 8 occasions to deal with major incidents. We had managed to provide support on every occasion but NPAS wanted some formal strategy in place to ensure there was never a failure to provide a base manager as an incident liaison in future scenarios. Upon further research, I discovered that these figures were not even correct. There had actually been 12 major incidents. Furthermore, it was clear that on every occasion there had been a base manager able to attend or available as a liaison.

I decided to write a report about my findings and about the feelings of my fellow base managers. I expressed that, on balance, I did not feel that the change to our working patterns would be justified by the eventual loss of expertise. I argued that the system we had in place had not failed, so there was no need to change it so drastically. Some people also have a tendency actively to seek out problems that simply do not exist. Some even purposefully manufacture trauma to that they can, in turn, be seen as the "hero", remaining unemotional and solving the issue, whilst others are thrown into chaos. This latter event is a worrying red flag that can alert us to narcissists.

My report was constructive in tone. Rather than simply demeaning the argument for change, I made other suggestions that could have provided that "safety net" that seemed to be the objective here, such as having base managers also obliged to be an "on call" roster in case of emergencies. Since we were only looking at one incident per month, and that we hadn't ever needed to call upon someone "on call" anyway, it was literally just a box-ticking safety net that would allow us to carry on as normal. There were also ways of staggering our shifts to ensure that cover was always available if necessary.

I sent my 14-page report off to Wakefield and awaited a response. Finally, I was told that my suggestions had been rejected. Specifically, I was informed that organisations should "not be run on goodwill"! I fundamentally disagreed with this statement. I would strongly argue that policing is very much dependent on goodwill. The goodwill of those working on the frontline who put into operation the systems that are devised by those within senior leadership.

I had been stonewalled several times before when I'd made suggestions to my superiors but on this occasion, I just couldn't let it go. I was deeply concerned about losing excellent members of staff if the changes went ahead. Although I knew it would ruffle feathers, I decided to write to the Chief Constable of West Yorkshire Police. As Martin Luther King said, "Sometimes you have to take a position that is neither safe nor politic, but one must take it because it is right." That's how I felt about it.

Well, it might have been the "right" thing to do in order to best serve my integrity, but it turned out to be the absolute *worst* thing to do for my career.

The can of worms that was opened as a result of that one email went on to end my police career. It began with me being called to a meeting in Wakefield, in April 2018, not to meet with the Chief Constable, but to be grilled by the Chief Operating Officer of NPAS. I later learned that I do not perform well in extremely stressful circumstances where there is an imbalance of power and injustice. I feel psychologically threatened. I also didn't know, at that point, that, being a non-linear thinker, I had a tendency to clash with linear thinkers because I had the ability to come up with creative solutions to complex problems that they would not see clearly, and rather view as me challenging their authority. This would inevitably force them into defence mode and resort to a default "command-and-control" approach, which further exacerbated the problem as I would feel shut down and dismissed. This resulted in me becoming disengaged with my work. This clash between linear thinkers in the management positions and non-linear thinkers in junior positions invariably leads to conflict. Once someone has been criticised and belittled, it is very easy simply to "turn up" for work, doing what is just necessary and then leave to go home.

The rest of 2018 and early 2019 became tainted with black clouds hanging over me as I attempted to navigate what became a particularly toxic environment. These negative experiences also caused me to become disillusioned with my role, which was a totally unnatural feeling for me. The weekly commute south on the M1 became a huge burden. At home, my behaviour and personality noticeably changed when, as each Sunday afternoon rolled around, I started to get my clothes and provisions ready and packed, dreading my 4.30am departure on the Monday morning.

When it was announced that the Lippitts Hill base was due to close in October 2019, with operations moving to a new base in Essex at North Weald, where there was no accommodation provision made for officers travelling from far away, I took the very difficult decision to bring my police career to a close. I was about to hit my 30-year anniversary in July 2019, so it felt as apt a time as any. I was ready for new challenges. As much as I loved aviation and the people that worked within it, perhaps it was time to move on.

I had already become fascinated in and started to study organisational psychology, and in particular how to beat bullying in the workplace. I took every opportunity I could to learn about organisational development – attending talks, seminars, and lectures, and reading up on the topic. I even started my own consultancy business. It soon became clear to me that my 30 years in policing had been my apprenticeship for a new and exciting career, upon which I could not wait to embark.

PART TWO:

LISTENING: CREATING A CULTURE OF PSYCHOLOGICAL SAFETY

CHAPTER FOURTEEN:

WHAT'S THE WORST THAT COULD HAPPEN?

Good leadership is about understanding and mitigating risk, and nowhere do you learn more about mitigating risk than when working with helicopters! But everything in life has risk attached to it. If you thought about everything going on in a helicopter, mechanically, and about all the things that could go wrong, you would probably never get into one. Many people decide this is not a thing they ever want to do! But then you think about the positive outcomes of being able to fly helicopters – getting people to hospital swiftly, people who would otherwise have died at the scene of an accident – and that most helicopters begin and end their journeys safely because of all the safety checks. Then you balance it out and say taking the risk is worth it. But if you only focused on the potential disasters, including all the infinite array of human errors that are possible, you'd never go anywhere.

We all deal with risk on a daily basis in our everyday lives. Some people attempt to eradicate risk altogether whilst others learn to live with it and simply reduce or mitigate it to a reasonable or manageable level. When I was working in police aviation, people would often say to me that they could never do what I do because it was extremely dangerous. But if I did a risk assessment on the relative risk of travelling 142 miles down the M1 motorway from my home in Staffordshire to Lippitts Hill and everything that might happen to me as a result of the number of other drivers I would pass on the way and the possible hazards, the greatest risk was actually the motorway driving! I knew that every helicopter I boarded was maintained to an extremely high level, that the pilots and crews were exceptionally well trained and that we had endless safety checks to reduce risk at every opportunity. That cannot be said about most of the cars on the road.

Risk is not a simple concept to understand, and it becomes even more complex when we view the "quantum risk" in a situation.

Tony Fish is an entrepreneur and author who is a pioneer in the digital space. He specialises in working with the plethora of data within an ever increasing uncertain, complex and ambiguous world. He cites a reoccurring and everyday problem being that there is too much data available to us; this creates "noise" and makes decision making an increasingly difficult process. This becomes ever more evident when we attempt to mitigate that risk. This creates the concept of "quantum risk" and Fish explains this in terms of three variables. Firstly, when you observe the same risk twice, it might look different or even disappear. Secondly, the same risk can be in many places simultaneously but still only count as one risk. And, finally, your risk and my risk directly affect each other across our data ecosystem, but they may be disconnected: in other words, they are coupled but may not be directly connected. He describes the concept of "quantum risk" as being somewhat complex and claims it "creates havoc with our existing frameworks and models".

I believe one of the greatest risks in life is to be unaware of your innate talents: both your psychological (cognitive) and psychomotor (how the brain works together with your physical actions, your reflexes, etc.) talents. If you don't understand what makes you tick, what your preferences are, what you are good at and what you are not so good at, what your mental strengths are, whether you are a linear or non-linear thinker, how you cognitively deal with and visualise complexity, and how detail-orientated you are, you can't deal effectively with the myriad situations you will find yourself in every day. And this will apply in both work or social settings. You may well think you are dealing with complex situations, but you may be coasting through life allowing others to steer you and control your behaviour. You may also react to situations in a way that sabotages your progress in life, or even your safety. We constantly need more understanding about our behaviours and how symptomatic they are of what goes on in our subconscious.

In aviation, we always have an added complexity: the need to mitigate risk in real time.

At CCAOU we had a well-worn routine when we changed over shift that involved a detailed briefing. The off-going crew would update the new crew about any tasks or events that had taken place or were likely to affect the next shift. For example, if there was a missing person still not located and the unit was awaiting updates as to where future aerial searches might be required. Or whether there were urgent tasks to complete that had to be conducted at a specific time for a specific reason. One of the tasks always conducted by the night shift, for example, was the request to search for evidence that hydroponics equipment was being used by households, which often meant they were growing marijuana!

During this very focused briefing, the two pilots who were handing over duties would also discuss any minor issues with the aircraft and how many hours were left to fly before a service was required. Weather conditions would also be discussed. Police air units have special dispensation to fly at lower weather limits than other commercial flying companies, so they have to watch weather briefings and updates very carefully.

The briefings would last for around 20 minutes and would include decisions being made about who would be seated where in the aircraft and the control room informed of this. We would also always rehearse the strict protocol that was to be followed in the case of a fire or loss of an engine during flight. There would also obviously be a physical fuel check. These were all elements of developing greater situational awareness.

Once this was all done, it would be a case of waiting for the phone to ring with a request for air support, at which point we would have to make a real-time assessment of whether all the conditions were suitable for us to be able to respond. Only moment by moment can risk be fully assessed and mitigated in aviation. No matter how much pre-planning is done, there is always the possibility of something out of the ordinary happening that had not been considered during the briefing; what you might call a "known unknown". (In risk management we say there are "known knowns", "known unknowns" and "unknown unknowns".)

For example, we were once asked to pick up an expert witness who was needed urgently for a murder trial. He had been travelling to Birmingham from the south west on the M5 and had become stuck in the backlog of traffic caused by a serious accident. The cost of delaying the murder trial had to be weighed against the cost of us flying to his location, picking him up and flying him to Birmingham. Next, we had to consider the weight of the passenger, and whether we would need to leave one crew member behind. Then we had to assess whether we had enough fuel for such a long round trip. We had to consider where we could land near the motorway, and whether we had maps ready with the pick-up and drop-off locations.

This is an example of a task that was received at base. If a request came in when we were already airborne, the set of circumstances became even more complex. There were even more factors to consider, and that is when teamwork and good synergy between team members was essential for making the best assessment and carrying out a successful operation.

Different scenarios throw up different complexity levels. The majority of tasks are "simple" on face value, but layers of complexity can come into play because individuals will see the same scenario differently, one person seeing it as complex, and the other seeing it as simple, so risk is a very difficult thing to be absolute about. When we talk about risk it is not purely an environmental risk that we need to be aware of, it is also the risk that we can so easily pose to ourselves if we do not possess self-awareness. We can easily forget that, individually, we are probably the most complex element of any system or process. As such, we are liable to create all kinds of unintended consequences due to our unique thoughts, ideas and actions.

CHAPTER FIFTEEN:

WHY DO THE WRONG PEOPLE END UP AT THE TOP?

In my 30-year police career, I built many strong and life-long friendships. I worked with kind, courageous and hardworking men and women and I always look back on my time in the police force with gratitude and a lot of happiness. It shaped who I am today. But I also saw many flaws in the leadership and organisational structure of the police force. I experienced an environment that allowed bullying to thrive in some areas and that didn't always value the perspectives and information that could be provided by officers "on the ground". On certain topics, respectful constructive criticism was shut down and a dangerously blinkered "official" narrative was allowed to dominate. This is what has become known as "cancel culture".

I believe that there are two factors at work here. Firstly, there is a technocratic desire to centralise authority and administration in the name of "efficiency". This occurs against and is justified by a backdrop of economic and political turbulence. Secondly a number of factors allow individuals ill-suited to leadership to rise up the ranks. People with fragile egos, who have a deep need to be proven right and get their own way, tend to create a toxic atmosphere that suffocates and paralyses discussion and debate, and subsequently creativeness and innovation. This can lead to poor decision-making, which can ultimately negatively affect our ability, as an institution, to serve the public.

It's a vicious circle and "perfect storm" scenario whereby increasing centralisation provides opportunities for career-driven individuals to be given positions that allow them to assert their authority over others, further diminishing the autonomy and voices of those below them.

So, what are the systemic factors at play that allow this self-perpetuating process to fester? In other words, why do the wrong people end up in positions of leadership and power?

There are so many factors at play. One very obvious one is described by a theory called "the Peter principle". This is a theory about managerial structure developed by Laurence J. Peter and explained in the book *The Peter Principle*, published in 1969, and co-authored by Raymond Hull. Even though it was ostensibly meant to be a satirical, it became widely read and gained great popularity, and does highlight a very real and serious problem.

The core concept suggests that people tend to be promoted to the "level of their own incompetence". In other words, within a typical organisation, people who do well at one job tend to be promoted. If they succeed in that job, they will be promoted again, and so on. The only time they don't get promoted and stay in a certain position is when they don't do the job well enough to be promoted to a higher level. But that means they don't do the job well enough to be in the position!

The Peter Principle describes the place where people end up as the "Peter Plateau" or the "Final Placement". If this was to happen in one or two cases in an organisation, then the rest of the workforce could probably shoulder the issues that would be created. The major issue happens when every employee throughout the hierarchy rises to the "level of their own incompetence". Then you have a real problem and the whole organisation is inevitably going to become pretty useless. This eventual state of stasis is referred to as "Peter's Corollary".

Another factor that can really compound this negative process is what is known as "The Dunning–Kruger Effect" which suggests that people who do not really have the skills to complete a task actually overestimate their ability to do it. This concept is based on research conducted by David Dunning and Justin Kruger in 1999 in which they observed that this assumed-but-delusional superiority was a form of cognitive bias. In their study 'Unskilled and Unaware of It: How Difficulties in Recognising One's Own Incompetence Leads to Inflated Self-Assessments' they found that this phenomenon tends to be exhibited by people who not only overestimate their own skills but also fail to recognise the expertise of other people as well as fail to see their own mistakes and lack of skill.

When you have the Peter Principle combining with the Dunning Kruger effect, you really do have the perfect storm because it suggests that, not only will you get people rising to positions in which they will be incompetent, they will actually fail to see they are incompetent, assume they are supremely competent and dismiss the input from others who do actually have the competence to help complete whatever task is at hand. This can all too easily lead to a toxic environment full of very arrogant incompetent people.

When looking at work output, it is also important to understand the Pareto Rule, which suggests that 80% of results are produced by 20% of causes. In other words, around 20% of drivers cause 80% of all traffic accidents, around 20% of factories produce 80% of pollution, and about 20% of employees are responsible for about 80% of the work output.

We need to understand and apply the Pareto Rule, in particular, when we consider the ratio of linear thinkers to non-linear thinkers, and the selection of leaders. It is thought that the majority of people – around 80% – are linear in their thinking, and thus only 20% are non-linear. The vast majority of leaders are selected purely on the basis of performance, personality and the ability to perform well during interviews. This favours linear thinkers, and thus linear-thinking people are promoted and become leaders. They inadvertently go from being an expert in their particular field (which requires linear thinking) to becoming a leader (which requires a non-linear perspective).

Good leaders need to have a bird's eye view (or "helicopter" view) of events, and good situational awareness, rather than a limited view or tunnel vision. When people are promoted above their level of ability, they will often battle on rather than reach for help. This can lead to burnout when they find themselves trapped in long days and uncomfortable situations. Sometimes, their anguish can go unnoticed until the worst happens… they develop health problems, their home life collapses, or they make critical mistakes.

The antidote to this requires individuals to become more self-aware, gain a greater understanding of complexity, and undergo regular monitoring of their mental health.

CHAPTER SIXTEEN:

WHY DO GOOD PEOPLE GET LEFT BEHIND?

"Diversity" and "inclusion" have become the buzzwords of modern culture, particularly in recruitment processes, but many people seem to have a narrow understanding of their true meaning; indeed, they can often be used to signal just the opposite of what they truly mean. Sadly, many people believe "diversity" only refers to accepting a range of different physical attributes. This is important, but it is even more important to ensure we accept a range of different thoughts and opinions, without "cancelling" people who disagree with us. Similarly, when we talk about "inclusion", this means including people in our conversations and in our workplaces regardless of whether they disagree with our thoughts and opinions. We may not bully people into a singular "world view". People have different perspectives based on their experiences and their religious beliefs. We have to learn to work with people even if they fundamentally disagree with our beliefs. We cannot force them to say something they do not believe. And we cannot exclude them if they oppose our beliefs. For this reason, we are not just looking to fill roles with a broad range of people based on their looks. Therefore, we cannot just fill quotas by checking off a list of identifying factors such as age, race and gender. As Matthew Syed says, in his recent ground-breaking book, *Rebel Ideas*, "You can't box-tick your way to real diversity."

If we want real diversity, if we want to make sure no one is "left behind", we have to have an agreement on what we mean by diversity. We have to define what it is and ensure we are all speaking the same language. Matthew Syed defines diversity as "cognitive diversity" and suggests that it will be the "key source of competitive advantage for the next 25—50 years", but only if people grasp and understand this fundamental concept. For this to happen, we need to become self-aware; we need to understand why we think what we think and then apply our thought processes to problem solving.

Syed uses the excellent example of the transformation of England's football team. After a long period of underachievement, manager Gareth Southgate turned to a diverse group to seek advice prior to the 2018 World Cup. The group of unpaid consultants were called the Football Association's Technical Advisory Board and included the educational theorist Michael Barber, serial entrepreneur Manoj Bedale, cycling coach Dave Brailsford, Sandhurst's first female commander Lucy Giles and Matthew Syed himself.

The sporting world was sceptical. How could a group lacking a technical understanding of football be of any value? But it was their ability to see things from such different perspectives and offer solutions never previously thought about that was their winning edge. They could not fall into an "echo chamber", which is often created when a group that are too myopically focused on the same thing from the same perspectives reinforces its self-perpetuating bias. Also, when you are in an unpaid advisory role, and you are meeting with other members of a group you'll be working with for the first time, you have nothing to lose by speaking up. Everyone can take the "10th Man" perspective. You don't have to force that contrarian point of view. As long as one person doesn't immediately push themselves into a position of authority, which can easily create a toxic culture, this set-up provides an environment that is psychologically safe by default. We have all sat in management or team meetings where everyone nods politely at the suggestions of a leader, even though we don't thoroughly agree. We usually do this when there is too much risk. It's not worth rocking the boat or jeopardising our job by suggesting a different way of thinking that might not be appreciated. Any time you have to ask yourself, "Is it safe to speak?" you know you are not working in a psychologically safe environment.

Cognitive diversity, or "diversity of thought", is perhaps the most relevant and most inclusive manifestation of "diversity". The way it is being emphasised these days in terms of the visible aspects of diversity – including race, skin colour, ethnicity and gender – is important, but these things are the superficial aspects of who we are. The thoughts and beliefs we have are far more important and fundamental. And these are the things that cause us to be challenged. We are complex individuals. All these aspects are obviously interrelated. Who we are on a cognitive level – our thoughts and feelings and beliefs – is directly affected by our social and cultural experiences and differences. We are shaped by our experiences every day so who we are can change over time. This is why true inclusion and real acceptance are so important. And this is also why it is so important for us to have true self-awareness. We need to know what creates bias and unhappiness, and to discover what innate talents we have to offer at work and in the community.

What we also have to be mindful of in these situations is the "initial condition sensitivity" of those forming the team or panel. What are their idiosyncrasies and biases? What mental state are they in at that moment? Are they linear thinkers or non-linear thinkers? How do they deal with stress? What is their current mental state? I liken it to a group of people entering an "escape room" game. Who, within the group, has the innate talents to read the situation, or to adapt to the environment, or to build complex relationships with the other members of the group? The whole group may well be going through the same experience, but they will ultimately all deal with the elements of the situation differently. Understanding these key facts is vital if the group are going to be successful and escape the room with friendships intact!

Leaders who know how to create psychologically safe environments will always get the best out of their team members. But they have to have the self-awareness to appreciate how difficult it can be for the people they are leading to speak up, that it is difficult for junior members of a team to challenge someone they perceive to be more senior, more experienced and better paid than them. A good leader downplays their superiority and goes out of their way to invite dissent. This is the only way to create a psychologically safe environment, which is an essential part of the process to reach cognitive diversity.

Gareth Southgate proved himself an excellent leader because he created an environment where he had gone out of his way to invite cognitive diversity. No one had an advantage in terms of knowledge base. They all had opinions based on their own specialist experiences, and those shone new light on old problems.

Another compounding factor could also be the element of "Conway's Law" at play. Or you could call this the "mirroring hypothesis". This is based on an argument put forward in 1968 by Melvin Conway, an American computer scientist and programmer. He suggested that, "Organisations which design systems are constrained to produce designs which are copies of the communication structures of these organisations." In other words, companies tend to create systems that mirror their own communication structures. If the communication is flawed, the company will be systemically flawed. Conway's Law is commonly associated with software development but is considered applicable to systems and organisations of all types.

There is plenty of debate around Conway's Law, and it has evolved over time, but it is still relevant today.

CHAPTER SEVENTEEN:
HOW DO WE BECOME BETTER LISTENERS?

I first became aware of the term "psychological safety" when I read *The Fearless Organization: Creating Psychological Safety in the Workplace for Learning, Innovation, and Growth* by Amy Edmundson, a professor in behavioural science at Harvard Business School. She describes it as, "a shared belief held by members of a team that the team is safe for interpersonal risk-taking" and expresses how it manifests in the belief that, "one will not be punished or humiliated for speaking up with ideas, questions, concerns or mistakes." In other words you will not be made to feel embarrassed or rejected for expressing views, even if they clash with someone else's views. She explains that psychological safety isn't about being "nice". Rather, it's about, "giving candid feedback, openly admitting mistakes, and learning from each other". She emphasises that this kind of organisational culture is increasingly important in the modern economy and that where there is real trust in the workplace, there are better results. She describes a psychological safe work environment as one where there is a "team climate characterised by interpersonal trust and mutual respect in which people are comfortable being themselves."

What I witnessed whilst working in police air support for 13 years, was that the process of centralisation and "top down" solutions – in other words, the removal of small autonomous units – actually eroded psychological safety. The more orders we received from "on high" and the less we were able to make our own decisions that were best for our small teams, the more mistrust there was, the more toxic the environment became. This in turn paralyses creativity and innovation. Good people become disengaged and are unwilling to develop their skills, and to articulate new solutions, because they do not feel they will be listened to or respected. They feel insignificant, like they don't have an input. When this happens, we end up seeing an unhealthy – and potentially dangerous – disconnect between the frontline team members and the senior leadership.

In 1989, a consultant called Sidney Yoshida developed the "Iceberg of Ignorance" concept, which suggests that, while 100% of information is known by those working on the frontline and closest to the customer, only 4% of that information actually reaches those within senior leadership. If that is the case, how can constructive solutions be found for those on the frontline if that information is being filtered out on its journey from the bottom to the top of an organisation? If solutions are to be found, organisations need to become much flatter and allow small autonomous groups of people to find those solutions. Leadership then becomes a means of serving those who hold the information with regards to both the problems and the solutions. Once you understand and appreciate this lack of flow of information, it is easy to understand why conflict and the subsequent disengagement of staff can result.

In 2014, the CAA introduced something called the "just culture" policy. This objective of this initiative was to encourage pilots and staff to report minor operational and procedural errors in an open manner so this could be shared to others in the organisation and lessons could be learned. Sounds great in theory but in practice it will never happen effectively unless you first have a foundation of trust. If you don't have that foundation, you are simply trying to impose a culture onto thin air, like building something on quicksand. It will quickly disintegrate.

The CAA's definition of "just culture" was: "A culture in which front-line operators or other persons are not punished for actions, omissions or decisions taken by them that are commensurate with their experience and training, but in which gross negligence, wilful violations and destructive acts are not tolerated." Ah, there's the sting in the tail! When pilots openly and in good faith reported incidents found themselves being investigated, and the threat of disciplinary action hanging over them – or even the possibility of being criminally prosecuted, this hardly encouraged others to follow suit. There was a negative knock-on effect. Well-intentioned staff, who could have reported incidents, which would have enabled learning and increased safety and the reduction of accidents, became reluctant to speak out. In aviation, retaining your pilot's licence is critical to remaining employed. If there was a potential threat to that, you are unlikely to report something. "Just culture" quickly destroyed the "trust culture"! If you do not trust your senior management not to take action against you, why would you ever put yourself in the firing line by reporting errors and problems?

Furthermore, how are you supposed to speak up when you believe there is a problem with the senior management? For a "just culture" to work, it has to be underpinned by psychological safety. There also has to be a genuine desire to resolve issues and learn from events in a non-judgmental setting. Senior managers need to have, or develop, the ability to listen – and to understand context and have good situational awareness of the whole picture. There can be no pointing of fingers or apportioning blame, only a desire to learn and to develop further understanding. There must be a deep appreciation that everything that is disclosed is done so on the basis of gaining knowledge and improving solutions. Of course, by default, this will also mean risk is mitigated, which – in aviation – is always critical. When a culture of psychological safety is maintained by leadership, everyone benefits from the honesty that is shared and the trust that is deepened and consolidated.

Only when senior management can hold themselves equally accountable to their staff and create an environment where their actions can be openly criticised, with respectful dissent and without fear of rebuke, is there true psychological safety. When senior management set themselves up in positions of power that exude the impression that they are untouchable, and that only they have the correct solutions to everything, that their role is simply keeping frontline staff in order, only a toxic atmosphere will persist.

If they are not aware of when their own functional illiteracies and dysfunctions create the issues experienced by those frontline staff, there will never be true psychological safety throughout the organisation. Once again, self-awareness is key to unlocking this barrier to psychological safety. Self-awareness not only helps the individual better understand their own behaviours, giving them insight into why they act as they do, it also provides a person with insight into why others behave in the way that they do. Self-awareness helps to bring context to situations that seem complex at first, but by seeking the root cause of the problem, can become simple. Chögyam Trungpa Rinpoche was one of the last great Dali Lamas to complete his training in Tibet before fleeing from the Chinese in 1959 and attending Oxford University in England. He said,

"The more you learn about your own mind, the more you learn about other people's minds. You begin to appreciate other worlds, other people's life situations. You are learning to expand your vision beyond what is just there in your immediate situation, on the spot, so your mind is opened that much more."

PART THREE:

SPEAKING: A POST-POLICE CAREER IN CONSULTING

CHAPTER EIGHTEEN:

CHANGE MANAGEMENT AND CONDUCT CHANGE

After leaving NPAS, I returned to my home police service of Staffordshire to serve out my remaining five months prior to my retirement in July 2019. Once again, I considered myself lucky. I spoke to the right people and rather than being posted to a custody suite I was allowed to use my training and crew resource management experiences within the world of organisational development: change management. I was amazed to discover that those experiences were transferrable. I had an excellent manager and a very different experience from the one I'd just come from.

When change is being implemented, the key building blocks are the individuals who will be affected. Success depends on how they are spoken to, listened to and understood. This is absolutely key to maximise engagement and reduce conflict. In fact, when individuals are nurtured correctly, conflict becomes an exciting and creative experience where solutions can be explored through cognitive diversity, within an environment of psychological safety.

The models of change management I learned about in this environment also allowed me to reflect on how and why the NPAS experiment had failed. They had simply forgotten about people and had become solely focused on the system. This basic failure and understanding is at the root of so many failed change projects. When we fail to appreciate the complexity of individuals and their needs, we cannot achieve good communication and teamwork. So we end up with a toxic environment where bullying is rife, lives become shattered, and no one wins. We get internal conflict and poor retention of staff and broken relationships. In terms of policing, that failure also equates to a breakdown of trust between the police and the public.

Another Peelian principle states: "Police, at all times, should maintain a relationship with the public that gives reality to the historic tradition that the police are the public and the public are the police; the police being only members of the public who are paid to give full-time attention to duties which are incumbent on every citizen in the interests of community welfare and existence."

If, within the police, we are not developing and nurturing constructive relationships with our fellow colleagues, how can those on the frontline be expected to build solid and sustainable relationships with the public? How can they show empathy and compassion to the public when their leaders and colleagues are not showing empathy or compassion towards them?

The biggest mistake that the leaders of NPAS made was not engaging with those on the frontline, not taking the time to understand what individuals were feeling and experiencing. The pilots and crew members who were affected knew exactly where the problems lay and also what the solutions were. A "well if you don't like it, you can always leave" mentality completely alienated people from the onset of the complex project and broke down any trust and engagement that projects such as these are reliant on. That "us and them" attitude, a concoction of over promotion and over confidence, immediately builds barriers that only grow bigger and higher, reinforced over time by people who are neither listened to, nor understood.

After retiring in July 2019, exactly 30 years to the day after I began my public service (I enjoyed the precision and symmetry), I took a month's break before returning to Staffordshire Police, in a civilian role, for a 12-month contract. As the Business Change Manager, I was commissioned with assisting the implementation of a computer-based record management system called "Niche". This new system was designed to be the very heart of the organisation, linking data from multiple sources to build a better record of criminal intelligence and events that would result in more informed decision making, all leading to improved public safety and order. I found my experience of training, leadership and crew resource management extremely useful as I helped implement the project. This project signified unprecedented change for many people within Staffordshire Police and there were many complex factors and pressures coming into play that would determine whether or not the implementation would be successful or unsuccessful.

With only a short delay, the project was delivered. I was then asked to research and deliver the Post-Implementation Review – more commonly known as the "lessons learnt" report. We were forever being told that we never learn from the past; if I could add some constructive oversight before leaving the police service, as my legacy, I felt that would be a positive thing.

The 32-page report covered such subjects as the project vision, the selection of project staff and the provision of change agents. My overriding conclusion was that the project's "successful implementation" was more to do with luck than good judgement. I also highlighted that people had different views of how "success" is measured. For some, success meant that when the system was switched on, it simply worked. For others, success would be if the system ultimately led to better provision of criminal intelligence and to keeping our communities safer whilst making life easier for frontline police staff. It was also hoped that the project would positively affect officer behaviours following its implementation.

The problem was, a "joint vision" of success is not possible without great communication. With such a wide spectrum of people, if they are not properly aligned in their vision, they will work to different agendas. I could clearly see why such a high percentage of digital transformations projects tend to fail.

Sadly – but not unexpectedly as I was seeing a running theme, I was never asked to elaborate or articulate on my findings to any senior officer before I departed in September 2020. I suspect the report is currently gathering dust in a drawer somewhere within the archives of Staffordshire Police. If I was offered the chance, I'd love to return to Staffordshire Police station and update the report after investigating how the staff feel about the system.

CHAPTER NINETEEN:

SELF-AWARENESS

My time at NPAS ended badly. Even with hindsight and through the lens of the self-awareness I gained, I could see, clearly, that I had been treated badly. I had done my best to communicate my concerns and had been met with nothing but negativity and disrespect. I was either stonewalled (not allowed to speak) or subjected to gaslighting (treated as if I had a psychological problem and was imagining things when, in reality, they were true.) The irony was that this terrible time ended up having a bad psychological effect on me. I became disengaged with my work, and resentful, angry and bitter. In particular, I developed zero tolerance for those who bullied others and was determined to do something with the rest of my life that would help empower those who are targeted by bullies. I could not cope with the injustice of what had happened to me. How could so many years of dedicated public service and passion for wanting to make a difference come to such an unpleasant ending? How did bullies always prosper and get away with physically and mentally harming others?

Shortly after leaving NPAS, I became involved in a group called "Conduct Change" and quickly became an ambassador. It was a great place to channel all that angst I'd been feeling. I was able to work alongside a group of similar-minded people who had all experienced workplace bullying and were seeking to make a real difference by defining workplace bullying through legislation. I grew increasingly active on LinkedIn and would reply fervently whenever I read posts and comments about workplace bullying, which I discovered was so prevalent and widespread. When "Conduct Change" gained charitable status, I became one of its trustees.

During this time, I also became extremely interested in organisational culture and began thinking deeply about what could be done to change it for the betterment of all individuals working within a team. I began to learn more about the nuances of leadership and psychological safety. I joined a group called the "Sustainable Leadership Foundation" and began to build a network of people who were exploring how to create better working environments where people could thrive rather than just survive. I read extensively on this topic and even started a Master's degree in Policing Leadership at Derby University.

As time went on, I became particularly focused on what we might do, on a practical level, to prevent workplace bullying in the first place. I kept thinking about one of the core Peelian Principles: "The test of police efficiency is the absence of crime and disorder, not the visible evidence of police action in dealing with it." I grew committed, then, to seeing workplace bullying eradicated, not just seeing the legal system dealing with it. I wanted to do something more proactive than simply waiting around to help pick up the broken pieces of people's lives in the aftermath of surviving workplace bullying. I also suspected that, if we tried to deal with it using threatening legislation alone, we might drive it more "underground" with bullies becoming more devious and covert in their actions.

I realised that the absence of workplace bullying altogether was our real measure of whether there was a good culture of psychological safety. If bullying was eradicated, it could only mean that a workplace was a good place to be, and that it could thrive and be prosperous.

One somewhat uncomfortable question that I had to ask myself was: what made people targets for bullying? How had I contributed, myself, to being in the line of fire (so to speak)? This felt even more important than the obvious question: what motivates the bully? Were bullies not also victims of the system that put them in positions of leadership when perhaps they weren't suited to them? A culture that allowed them to be promoted to a level they did not have the innate talent to deal with? We all know that "with great power comes great responsibility" but if you're not cut out for the responsibility, you're obviously going to abuse the power.

I decided to do some self-development work, which included a psychometric assessment. I was allowed to "speak to myself" through a non-judgemental process with no apportioning of blame or pointing of fingers. This was a fascinating and unique experience that allowed me to break down and examine my cognitive abilities, my preferences and my psychomotor skills. I was able to look at my experiences through this lens and put them into the context of who I am. It helped me understand why I had felt bullied, which then allowed me to heal, forgive and move on. It was life changing.

My new insight into myself helped me understand why I behaved in certain ways, and why I had become so disengaged, frustrated and disillusioned in my role. I looked at my behaviour within the context of my own innate talents, including my biases and preferences. I began to understand why these negative experiences and my own innate talents had been reflected in my response to the situation, and then how those behaviours had negatively affected those around me.

Through this process, I was even able to look at the whole situation from the perspective of the bully. I considered what their life might have been like. What was their personal situation? What pressures were they themselves being placed under, at work and at home? Were they a victim of a system that actively allowed, and even encouraged, people to become over promoted – rendering them unwittingly incompetent in their job? As a result of this, did they become desperate to prove to others around them, and the people who promoted them, that they were more than capable of successfully fulfilling the role even though they felt completely overwhelmed by it? Had they become trapped in the financial success? Were they afraid of losing the benefits of promotion? Did they have a fragile ego that would not allow them to admit they were incompetent?

The more work I did, and the more insight I gained, the more I felt able to forgive and move on. The dark days were behind me and I evolved into a better, more confident version of myself. I then found that new-found confidence reflected in my behaviours and actions.

Through this process, I got great insight into why bullies become bullies. And I began to believe it was because they were once bullied themselves but had not been able to process it and do the necessary self-development. When hurt, people often seek retribution and revenge. But they are unable to take their revenge out on the person or people who bullied them. Thus, they will take it all out on people junior to them. Doing this is counterproductive as it accelerates a physical and mental downwards spiral. Harbouring resentment, hate and anger hurts innocent people.

I also grew to understand that personal development and change does not require huge behavioural alterations and big sacrifices. Usually only a few, small adjustments are required. It's like if a free-flowing river had become blocked by 100 logs strewn across its path, creating a blockage and preventing that free flow of water. You would not need to move every single log, which would require a huge amount of energy and time. If you stand still and take the time to observe and assess the situation, you will work out, strategically, which one or two logs to remove. Once the water is flowing again, the other 98 logs will start to move and flow down the river, removing the blockage. By slowing down and considering the best strategy, we speed up the whole process and conserve effort and time.

Organisational efficacy can only benefit from teaching self-awareness and combining that with innate talent discovery, paying close attention to the level of complexity required for the role and ensuring a candidate's aptitude for complexity matches that. The higher up an organisation a person rises, the more they must be able to deal with complexity, which includes helping others under their management find the positions they are best suited to. When an organisation has people well suited to their roles in terms of talent, there is better employee retention, reduced employee sickness, a heathy culture of psychological safety, fewer disputes and an all-round better work environment. And there are resultant knock-on benefits such as reduced recruitment costs and training costs, and increased wellbeing, which leads to better engagement, more creativity and accelerated innovation. As a result of this alignment a culture in which people can thrive is created organically; such a culture is thus a by-product of a healthy process rather than something that is continually "chased" by leaders, who generally cannot fathom out the root causes for a failing organisation and continually throw "darts in the dark" in an attempt to find solutions.

When individuals become more self-aware, it not only benefits the individual but also has a positive impact on those around them. When we become more self-aware, we also become more aware of the circumstances of others, our general empathy increases, our involvement and investment in our surroundings grows deeper, and we look more closely at how and why people behave in the way they do. We start to look beyond visual behaviours, which are often the symptomatic reactions to deeper and more subconscious factors. Self-awareness helps us understand more of the root causes of disputes. For example, it may help us not to take things personally. Rather than become paranoid that the issue is all about us, we can depersonalise it and look at it more holistically and objectively, from a non-judgmental perspective.

With more self-awareness, I was able to look at my experiences in a whole new light; I got a much healthier perspective on things that had previously deeply upset me.

After I stopped working for the police altogether, in September 2020, and started working on my own projects, I grew to understand how vitally important self-awareness is in order to ensure that we choose the right career path for ourselves. If we do not base our career choices on our innate talents and preferences, we will end up on the wrong path, which is bad for us and bad for everyone around us. Conversely, when we are well-suited to our career path and level of managerial responsibility, we can ensure that our team members are given the right opportunities and we can encourage them to apply for roles that best suit their talents and preferences.

Self-awareness is not a one-time crash course; it is an ongoing process. Learning about yourself constantly is important, especially in the police. Police officers need to remain open-minded and vigilant, observing and learning from their own responses to a diverse range of situations, from their colleagues' behaviours, and from all the nuances and complexities of human nature they get to observe and experience when they come in contact with members of the public.

Police officers are exposed to so many different events. The potential for trauma is endless and quite different from, say, the trauma that army officers can expect. For a police officer, a traumatic experience could be around the corner at any moment of any given day, and there is no telling in what form it might come. Any radio message might be a call that requires a critical response, and a life-or-death decision might be called for. Every police officer will have a different "initial condition sensitivity" at the time they are called upon to take critical action. Their mental state, including any PTSD they are carrying over from past events will affect their decision making, will have an impact on the risk posed to their colleagues and members of the public. If they are unaware of their own psychological state, if they don't have self-awareness, that risk is hugely increased.

Self-awareness is all about having an understanding of the events and experiences from our past that have shaped us, as well as an appreciation of our innate talents and preferences. Increased self-awareness is the key to better decision making in all our future endeavours. When we know ourselves on a deep level, we will get better outcomes for ourselves and for others around us – whether they be in our professional lives or personal lives. Increasing our self-awareness will always mitigate risk and allow us to achieve our full potential, protecting ourselves and others along the way.

CHAPTER TWENTY:

HUMAN ANALYTICS – A PERSONAL USER MANUAL?

Imagine if we all possessed our own personal "user manual"; we would certainly be much better placed to protect our own mental health and, as a result, make better and more carefully considered decisions within each the situation we find ourselves in. We would have better judgement about when we might need to reach out for help. We would not fear being vulnerable because we would better understand where our vulnerability came from.

Unfortunately, even when we are given a user manual, we are often not very good at using it. Consider the bulky user manual that comes with a new piece of technology – a TV, for instance. How many of us throw away the full manual, happy just to refer to the single "quick setup" sheet? We are satisfied to know enough to produce a picture on the screen. Why bother with the more intricate details? We don't think about it until a problem occurs and we realise we've thrown away the instructions and don't know what to do. Perhaps there are time constraints being placed upon us and we wish to obtain a picture as quickly as possible. Perhaps we are being watched and scrutinised or being pressurised by younger family members to "just make it work". Not wishing to show our vulnerability, we blunder on, hoping that all the cables and plugs are all in the right sockets. We know we will eventually switch the TV on and it will probably spring to life, but our success is often as much down to faith and luck than anything we have actively contributed to the exercise. We should and could know more about the full list of features of this new appliance, but we are not prepared to invest the time or energy to study it. How many times have we convinced others that we know exactly what we are doing but subconsciously we are simply praying that that all goes well, unconvinced of our own abilities? This is most likely the "Dunning-Kruger" effect in action, where people with low ability, expertise, or experience regarding a certain type of task or area of knowledge can overestimate their ability or knowledge. This is the basis of cognitive bias.

How often do we do the same thing in life? We are all too quick to dismiss or throw away the potential user manual we could access if we had more self-awareness. We could do so much more if we invested time into learning more about ourselves. Unfortunately, we are more than happy to blunder on because we would rather not appear vulnerable. We desperately do not want to be seen as ignorant as that would seriously dent our precious egos. We are taught so many basics as children, how to talk and walk, how to eat, and be polite. But we are rarely taught enough about how we think, about how we respond and adapt to ever changing and fluid situations, about how to observe and consider the environments we find ourselves inhabiting and consider why we behave as we do in those unique and continuously changing circumstances. The world would probably be a much better place if we all learnt this self-awareness from an early age and continued learning it as we progressed in life.

Just imagine if each police officer had their very own personal user manual. They would be far better equipped to survive the rigours of what is a complex and demanding career. Those demands – that come in both mental and physical forms – are borne not only by the officers themselves, but by all those they interact with, including their colleagues, their family members, friends and loved ones, and members of the public. Knowing, ahead of time, how we will respond in certain situations, might affect our decisions, including whether or not we are even suited to a career in the police. If we had that personal insight, we might reconsider joining, we might delay an application until the timing was better, or we might focus on a certain career path that we feel we would be best suited to. And from the perspective of our managers, they could make better decisions as to our suitability for promotion and leadership or supervisory roles.

There are people who – by virtue of their specific psychometric profile – should not join the police. This would be the optimum decision for both them and all who might be affected by them. There are also those who are not suited to positions of authority. If we had much better self-awareness, we would know this ahead of time and we wouldn't end up with the wrong people in leadership and supervisory roles, thus we would avoid toxic situations like workplace bullying, from arising. Psychometric analysis, when done well, is actually a vital component of recruitment and promotion; it helps managers to understand a person's ability to deal with complexity, and then align it with the complexity required for a specific role.

Some psychometric assessments depend on the observation of behaviours and personality. The one I took went deeper and asked why those behaviours were displayed in the first instance. It examined the prevailing circumstances and the environment in which they were enacted. It considered context and complexity. It built up a detailed cross section of who I was by acknowledging the intrinsic connection between three vitally important elements:

> **Cognitive ability** (related to the MIND): how do we deal and cope with thinking about and analysing complexity?
>
> **Psychomotor abilities** (related to the BODY): relates to how our brain controls our physical actions.
>
> **Internal preferences** (related to our SPIRIT): relates to our preferences and how we like to do things – i.e. whether we are a doer, a thinker, a leader or an administrator.

If we can map out these fundamental, core elements for each individual, we can provide opportunities within a role that best suits their level of complexity, which will increase their chances of success and of gaining fulfilment and purpose. We can reduce burnout and mental-health issues because we can save people from falling into the trap of over confidence or even incompetence. When we apply Tony Fish's definition of "Quantum Risk" we can start to identify the specific risks each individual possesses and how those risks manifest as behaviours.

Another vital factor in human analytics is to remember that we cannot remove the impact of our personal and social lives. They are intrinsically linked. If we create better workplace environments and experiences that will ultimately reflect within a person's home and social life, and vice versa.

Something that emerged in my assessment, that didn't surprise me too much, was that I was found to be creative, with a particular enjoyment for problem solving. I was also inquisitive and on the non-linear scale. I saw and visualised things differently from someone who thought in a linear way.

Linear thinking is a process of thought following known cycles or step-by-step progression, where a response to a step must be elicited before another step is taken. Non-linear thinking – also described as "lateral thinking" is the ability to think through things in multiple different ways and look at things from many different perspectives, rather than thinking in a step-by-step process in one direction and based on the concept that there are multiple starting points from which one can apply logic to a problem. The split in the population in terms of who is non-linear and linear is estimated to be around 20—80, with 20% of us being non-linear, and the other 80% being linear thinkers. This can create issues and conflict if it is not properly understood, as linear leaders have a tendency to push back against those who are non-linear when offered solutions, especially if there a non-linear thinker is junior to an over-promoted linear thinker. Solutions that appear simple and obvious to a non-linear thinker can often appear nonsensical to a linear thinker.

I had some awareness of the fact that I was a "creative" in the past and had always seen this trait as being a positive thing. Within my assessment I discovered that it can actually be a weakness, even an "Achilles' heel". I have a tendency, when difficulties arise at work or home, to see a way through the issue that seems very simple to me and so I often rush to articulate my ideas. However, those ideas are often innovative and novel, so they cannot be well understood by linear thinkers. In my excitement and caught up in my passion, I can alienate people by bombarding them with my enthusiasm before they have a chance to absorb the details. If this is a work-based situation and I am presenting what I perceive to be my "brilliant" solution to someone who ranks higher than me in an organisation, they might feel threatened and challenged, and even embarrassed to have had a lower-ranked colleague "solve" a problem that was their responsibility. This can unfortunately and needlessly lead to conflict. If this negative form of conflict occurs, the person in the position of power or authority will likely adopt a command-and-control position to protect their status. This situation benefits no one as the opportunity to solve the problem can be lost in the heat of the conflict. Whenever I experienced this stance and the fallout, I would become frustrated and disengaged, which depressed me even further as I cared so passionately about my job.

With hindsight I can now see that my exuberant behaviour and creativity may have brought out the worst in more senior members of staff. In the process of rejecting my solutions that – being linear thinkers – they did not compute, they would feel threatened. This was a sad misunderstanding. I was not after their job, nor was I attempting to show them up in any way, I simply wanted to solve the problem.

The spiral continued when I received criticism which I perceived as being unfounded. I would take the criticism personally and feel bullied, at which point I would start to withdraw, which would affect my home life as well as my work life. Once I withdraw, I suppress my natural abilities to be inquisitive and solve problems. So, ironically, I am the one I hurt the most, as well as the people closest to me.

Following my psychometric assessment, I realised that I had played an active part in the situation where I felt bullied. I did not understand, well enough, how I operated. I now know that, as a non-linear thinker, I assess a situation and visualise solutions in a different way from linear thinkers. I learnt that differences between people exist naturally and we all need a deeper understanding of each other if we are going to come up with the best solutions. When we understand ourselves better, conflict can actually aid problem solving. On some level, it is actually amazing to think that we assume we are all speaking the same language. I now know that, even when we use the same words, we don't necessarily speak the same language! If we cannot communicate the solution that we visualise, we may as well be speaking a different language altogether. This is at the root of so much conflict and discord.

I now have a much clearer understanding of why conflict was created during the restructuring of police air support under NPAS. The recruitment of crew and pilots actually encourages and promotes people of a more non-linear thinking. They need to be curious and self-motivated; they need to be problem solvers. They are sometimes being expected to think in an innovative way in order to solve big problems in real time. We were unwittingly selecting from the 20% of the population who have a non-linear perspective. When these non-linear thinkers challenge the more linear minded leaders who are implementing change, we inadvertently create friction and conflict as the linear minded leaders feel both challenged and threatened. Rather than seeking to understand, they unfortunately default to a command-and-control position of "I have the rank so just do it!" Only by appreciating each other's thinking can we build psychologically safe environments where everyone can speak up, knowing they will be respected and listened to.

This psychometric analysis helped me understand that the root cause of the bullying I experienced towards the end of my time with NPAS was as much my doing as anyone else's. I did not understand myself well enough to understand that I posed a direct risk to myself. And as a result, I experienced real mental trauma and the physical symptoms that accompany that. I had to see my doctor on a number of occasions complaining of painful stomach cramps, which he believed were related to the stress and anxiety I was experiencing. You can't really separate physical and mental trauma; they always go hand-in-hand. One precipitates the other.

Ideally, if we want to gain the deepest and most beneficial insight, a psychometric analysis should be obtained from our subconscious. Allowing us to "talk to ourselves" in a non-verbal sense. Traditionally we gain these insights from third parties, but because they are only basing their assumptions on the observation of behaviour, this can easily be biased and be heavily flawed as a result. In my probationary years of policing, my annual performance review would be written by my sergeant and then sent up through the ranks to my divisional commander, a chief superintendent. A common comment was "PC Howell is a quiet officer". It was written as if this "quietness" was a negative. Yes, I was quiet in those early days but what does that actually mean and what was causing that quietness? Nobody ever took the time to ask or investigate as to why I was quiet.

Behaviours are symptoms and consequences of what is happening deep within us, reflecting all the things that have gone into creating who we are – our innate talents and our experiences. "PC Howell is a quiet officer" is an observation, it is not critical analysis; it lacks context, which is a vital ingredient.

It is ironic that the police service puts such a high price on investigation and yet doesn't fully investigate the potential of their own people.

We all need a psychologically safe environment in which to "speak to ourselves". We require a holistic non-algorithmic approach where we are unable to lie to ourselves or manipulate the findings. We need a process that allows us to contextualise our previous behaviours and actions, and then carry these findings with us going forward, providing us with a layer of protection from the events that will inevitably strike us in the future. Developing this self-awareness allows for a root-cause analysis of events, therefore further reducing the risk of failure or suffering down the line.

I believe we need to take specific action to acquire the level of self-awareness necessary for us to function at our best, and for the betterment of those around us. We have to make a concerted effort. It will not simply come to us as a result of a passive process. Left to our own devices to find, understand and interpret ourselves we are exposed to too much bias. In my case, I thought that I was creative, able to understand and solve problems whilst fighting injustice, but this unwittingly became my Achilles' heel. I had to learn after the fact where my weaknesses were. Having this knowledge ahead of time would have saved me so much anguish. Too many people never grasp the importance of human analytics, of assessing themselves and deepening their self-awareness *before* making all-important life choices and critical decisions. When we don't understand and appreciate our inherent idiosyncrasies and our innate talents, we cannot seek out the best opportunities in life that will give us purpose and allow us to flourish.

Human beings are not machines. As much as you try to understand the human condition, there will always be surprises. But that doesn't mean to say we shouldn't try to be as aware as possible. And the best place to start is with ourselves. The more we truly understand about our own behaviours and all the things that influence us, the more we will understand about others. You may believe that you can't possibly know how you would respond in a certain situation, but we can actually go a long way towards predicting that. If you know where to find the information and how to interpret it, you can start to build a quantum picture of who you are. We all have the potential to own our personal instruction manual. This will give us a much better moment-by-moment insight into why we respond in a certain way in any given situation. Nowhere could this be more useful than in the police service.

EPILOGUE:

THE FUTURE OF POLICING

At the time of writing, policing in the UK seems to be in a state of flux and everyone has an opinion on it. It is under the microscope and at a critical crossroads. You could argue that policing is always under the microscope, which is to be expected, as the state of our police service affects us all; we all have a vested interest in it. But the ways of achieving change need as much scrutiny as anything else. Constant calls for our leaders to be sacked and replaced don't address the systemic problem – that we are appointing the wrong leaders in the first place. "Knee-jerk" reactions are not constructive or productive in the long term.

After dodging bullets for many years, the Met Police Commissioner, Cressida Dick, resigned in February 2022. She was finally caught in the crossfire between a Conservative Home Secretary and a Labour Mayor of London, but she was also accused of not addressing systemic failures within the Met police that led to toxic environments festering and scandals emerging. I have no doubts that the new Met Commissioner, once selected, will announce that they will be "changing the culture". But if they continue being advised by the very same "experts" who failed to help their predecessor, I don't know how things can change.

I also feel alarmed by the policing of information and expression. Cancel culture is toxic, and the idea that the sharing of any information should be criminalised is chilling and I hope this idea goes nowhere. We cannot have a civilised society and a democratic political system if people are not allowed to dissent, to expose fraud, and to debate. Without diversity of thought and opinion, without transparency of factual information, we cannot evolve. We need the exact opposite of what is being proposed in things like the "Online Safety Bill". We need an open forum and a psychologically safe environment so that people can speak up and be listened to. And the police need to have a role in shaping that environment. To use a musical term, policing needs to be ahead of the beat (no pun intended), not behind it. Or, as they say in many sports. Get to where the ball is going, not to where it currently is.

Albert Einstein said, "We cannot solve our problems with the same thinking we used when we created them." So, we need to look at *how* we think, not *what* we think. If we have always tried to solve our problems with linear thinking, and that hasn't worked, then let's have a go at solving our problems with non-linear thinking. Let's have a better understanding of the complexity of problems and appreciate that simple, top-down solutions do not work.

I also believe that, fundamental to our success is a full-scale increase in self-awareness. It is absolutely logical that when we understand our own unique and innate talents, as well as our preferences and biases, we will make better choices from the opportunities offered to us. Our world is becoming increasingly complex and difficult to manage. We must nurture leaders who can deal with complexity, and who have the humility to listen to the teams they manage. They must be able to navigate the political and social pressures that are imposed upon them and find the best solutions. In policing, in particular, the creep of what we call "the surveillance state", the increasing influence of corporate power on our institutions, and the weakening of community and family connections through dehumanising technology, all threaten to undermine trust in police. Now, more than ever before, we need to foster direct and closer relationships between police officers and members of the public. We will only achieve this if we appoint leaders who have this vision.

When we match the right people to the right roles, when we ensure that non-linear thinkers complement linear thinkers, when we ensure we are all possessed with the self-awareness to know when to speak and when to listen, we end up with a psychologically safe environment, and we will prosper. A psychologically safe environment fosters cooperation, trust and understanding. These values are at the core of the Peelian principles that Sir Robert Peel proposed back in 1829, and they need to be at the core of the future culture of policing.

NOTE TO READER

I am passionate about sharing this knowledge and helping people achieve better self-awareness, because I firmly believe it is the key to eradicating workplace bullying. Indeed, I feel positive about all the experiences and skills I can bring to a wide variety of organisations. If reading about my experiences and what I learnt from them inspires you, and you believe that I could further help your organisation, I hope you will get in touch. I still have a burning desire to be of service, and to continue to learn on the job.

Find me at:
www.ableandrush.com

Email:
david.howell@ableandrush.com

LinkedIn:
https://www.linkedin.com/in/david-howell-aa9196115/

ACKNOWLEDGEMENTS

When I first entered into this venture, I really didn't know what I was getting into, but with the support of loving family and friends, I managed to get to the end and produce something that I am proud of. In fact, it has been a very similar experience to the journey I undertook when I entered the police service, starting out naïve and inexperienced but enthusiastic, and learning on the job. I am immensely grateful to my wife, Elaine, for her patience and support, and to my daughters Abbie, Elsie and Izzy, who are with me in spirit every step of the way in all I do. I could have filled a whole chapter thanking all of the fascinating characters and inspirational mentors I have had the pleasure of serving with during my time in the police service. I feel privileged to have been able to call them colleagues. Many of them are mentioned within the book but those who are not, I am no less indebted to. I would like to thank my dear friends, Junior and Melissa Schoeman, who have inspired and encouraged me in all my endeavours, and helped shape the person I have become today. My huge thanks to everyone at Couper Street Books, especially Dan Prescott and Claire Wingfield for their skills and professionalism, and a very special thank you goes to my long-suffering, patient and exceptionally skilled editor, Susannah Saary. With her insight and talent, we turned a collection of random stories about my experiences into a book that will hopefully bring a new perspective on policing to many readers. Finally, I must thank my mum and dad who always supported me, even when they didn't wholeheartedly agree with the particular path I chose! Mum, this book is for you.

David Howell was born in 1967 in Staffordshire. He joined Staffordshire Police Service in 1989 and served for 30 years, working in Stoke-on-Trent, Lichfield and London. He was part of the Central Counties Air Operations Unit which became NPAS in 2013. When he left the police in 2019, he started a career in leadership and change management. He now has a consultancy company called Able and Rush (People Solutions) Ltd, which offers bespoke training in leadership and teamwork. *Speak Up, Listen Down* is his first book. It is a candid account of his experiences in the police service and his struggle with bullying in the workplace, which he now actively campaigns against.

Printed in Great Britain
by Amazon